## ALSO BY ROSE MARIE CALICCHIO DUNPHY

*Orange Peels and Cobblestones*, a novel based on a true event.

*Ciottoli e Bucce D'Arancia*, the Italian translation of the above novel.

*That First Bite-Chance or Choice*, co-written with Mary Sullivan, r.c. non-fiction, about eating disorders using the 12-Step Program of AA.

THE SCENT OF ITALIAN COOKING
Copyright@2014 by Rose Marie Calicchio Dunphy

All rights reserved. Printed in the United States of America.

For information email Tea Leaf Publishing,
tealeafpublishing@gmail.com

Photographs @2014 by J. Dunphy

Design by Rose Marie Calicchio Dunphy

ISBN 13:  978-1500915674
       10   150091567X

# The Scent of Italian Cooking

Rose Marie Calicchio Dunphy

*This book is dedicated to all the women in my life who taught me how to cook and to love cooking - my grandmother, mother, mother-in-law, aunts, cousins. Also, to many of my male relatives who are as competent in the kitchen as they are in the work they do for a living.*

# Table of Contents

Introduction

Shopping for Food

Appetizers — Page 1

Soups & Salads — Page 9

Pasta — Page 17

Pesce or Seafood — Page 29

Carne or Meat — Page 40

Sauces — Page 58

Vegetables — Page 63

Rice & Potatoes — Page 70

Bread(Pane) & Pizza — Page 76

Desserts (Dolci) — Page 87

   Index — Page 115

# INTRODUCTION

When I first started to cook, I was 22 years old and newly-married. All I knew how to make was French toast. But I watched my mother-in-law cook very simple and basic dishes and learned. I read recipes in newspapers and cookbooks and tried them. I remembered my past (see my published novel, ORANGE PEELS and COBBLESTONES) and the meals my grandparents in Italy made and, later those of my mother's, where there was a mine of delicious dishes prepared easily with fresh ingredients and the love of food and family that Italians display so well. I asked other family members and friends for recipes. Over the years, I've accumulated an arsenal of recipes and the confidence to know that I can cook anything, even leftovers, and make it taste delicious.

### Cooking Better than You Think

With the proliferation of so many cooking shows, you'd think that you would find every man, woman and child in the kitchen practicing the art.

But hardly anyone cooks at home any more. Eating out is the norm rather than the exception. And if not eating out, people buy meals prepared by others from a takeout restaurant or supermarket rather than cook their own. Also, the family rarely eats at the dinner table all together as in the past. Mothers and fathers grab bites usually in front of the TV or behind the wheel and in shifts as they rush to a child's soccer practice, dance lesson or some other errand.

What's the point of watching cooking gurus if it doesn't translate into learning from them and putting the new-found knowledge into practice? We've become voyeurs rather than doers; couch potatoes, watching sports rather than playing them or taking a course in art or music appreciation instead of one where you actually paint, draw or play an instrument.

The present generation, which is into so much fun, doesn't know the fun they're missing. The fun is in the cooking, not just in the eating.

When I cook, I'm mesmerized. Onions that sauté in olive oil or chicken legs and thighs that brown in the skillet delight my nostrils. Strips of red, green or orange peppers, string beans, yellow or green zucchini blended with purple eggplant and sprigs of parsley create a canvas fit for Rembrandt. Pasta rolling in boiling water, ready to be drained and topped with spoonsful of tomato or pesto sauce becomes springtime forever. And when I make bread, working the rising and baking times around my schedule, the textures, smells send me reeling in euphoria. The contentment and satisfaction I feel knows no bounds.

Like wood that heats us twice – once when it's cut and again when it's burned – cooking feeds us in multiple of ways.

-It's healthier both in mind and body. You control the ingredients, their quantity, quality and freshness. And there's no one to boss you around or tell you that what you're doing is wrong.

-It's social and can be a cooperative effort open to spouses, friends, children or grand-children and bring you closer to them.

-It's cheaper. What you chop, assemble and cook for yourself costs less than store-bought meals and it leaves you more money for other necessities or enjoyments.

-It's better for the environment. Potato peels decompose while plastic containers do not and you help to save our planet.

-It's creative to try different combination of flavors and colors and pleasing to the eye. It's why we love to see pictures of food.

But where's the time to cook, you ask? You work, you have a family. You're just too busy!

I wonder if we realize how much time is squandered checking email, talking on the phone or watching television. Surely there could be a half hour or hour found to prepare a home-cooked meal. Or, we could cook more on weekends to carry us through one or two days mid-week. Since we live such a fast-paced life, the key then is to choose our priorities and enjoy life and make it as healthy, happy and as long as it can possibly be. A good friend of mine, Tony, always takes me back when he reminds me, "This is not a dress rehearsal. We only pass through this life once." How important to make the most of it!

Another friend, Vince, says, "The best memories I have of my childhood are walking into my grandmother's kitchen. It was like entering heaven. All my senses were stirred and I became alive."

For many of us, our senses were stirred and we became alive when we entered our mother's or grandmother's kitchens. The aroma of food cooking on the stove or baking in the oven intoxicated us, overwhelming us with joy and building a tradition of lasting memories of the people who loved us. For me it also includes the kitchens of my Italian relatives in Italy. Every time I visit my aunts, uncles and cousins, or they visit me, it's in the kitchen where we congregate. In the kitchen our minds, mouths and eyes feast on the most delicious food and drink that the earth can provide and our human hands can prepare. It is where we are family, where we become one.

I want to continue this tradition for my children and grandchildren and for others who wish it – to stir their senses, for them to become alive, not just at holiday times but every day or as many days of the year as possible.

For this reason, I am collating my family's favorite recipes into this cookbook so they can live on not only in our kitchens, but also in our hearts and souls and senses and in those of our children.

*Rose Marie Calicchio Dunphy*

The House and Street where I was born in Castellaneta, Italy

# Shopping for Food

When male friends and family found out that I was writing a cookbook, a number of them asked me to include some information about how to shop for food, especially for vegetables and meats.

"How do you tell when they're at their freshest and at their best quality? How do I know which to pick?" asked my brother-in-law, Bob. Widowed a few years ago, he now has to shop and cook for himself after many years of enjoying his wife's wonderful cooking.

At first I thought this a silly question. It's common sense to know it, I felt. After all, we grew up in families where food shopping was done, where our mothers or someone else cooked. But then, I remembered an incident a few years back when we were having company for dinner and I was making a wonderful meal of codfish sautéed in fresh herbs, rice, asparagus and salad. At the last minute, I wanted to include some mushrooms sautéed with onions as another side or to mix with the rice, so I sent my husband to the nearest market to buy a package of mushrooms. He often accompanied me when I shopped, so I trusted him. When he returned, I couldn't believe my eyes. He presented me with the blackest, most wilted mushrooms I'd ever seen!

"But they look black when you cook them. I purposely searched for the blackest ones they had," he said in his defense. Needless to say, I skipped the mushrooms that night.

So for you, Bob, and for all the people who eat out or order food in and/or don't know or have forgotten what raw food looks like, I will include a few words here about how to choose the best foods for quality and nutrition.

**Fresh vegetables** should feel firm to the touch and be free of cuts, bruises and brown, black or yellow spots. **Green** vegetables like **string beans, asparagus, broccoli (some is purple), peppers (they come in all colors) etc. should have a vibrant color, green or otherwise, and you should hear the "snap, crackle or pop" when you break them.** Again, no spots or cuts on the skin. **Leafy greens** like **swiss chard, spinach, broccoli rabe and lettuce** should also be a vibrant green, with no spots or wilted look. Other colored vegetables like **eggplant** should also be firm and have the maroon color with no spots or lesions. If you buy firm vegetables and discover some spots on them, simply cut off the damaged part.

**Mushrooms,** unlike the ones my husband bought**,** should be white or gray depending on variety and firm to the touch. **Tomatoes,**

which come in red or yellow, should also be firm, with no spots or breaks. The same is true for all **fruits**, except those that are soft, like fresh figs. However, some fruits like pears and peaches taste sweeter when they are a little soft to the touch because they are ripe.

Be sure to **wash thoroughly** all fruits and vegetables before using to eliminate any pesticides or bacteria that may be left after picking and handling. It's always **best to buy in season** and summer is the best season for most areas.

**Meats** should also be bought at their freshest, so always **check the date** that they are packed. Although meats are dyed to give them more red color, look that they aren't brown (from oxidation) and don't have too much fat and grizzle. Some marbling within is desirable, especially on beef, as this makes it more flavorful and tender. To **tenderize beef (steak),** make a marinade of oil, vinegar and spices, pour over meat, cover and refrigerate from a few minutes to a couple of days.

Develop a **friendly relationship with the butcher** whether it's at the supermarket or at the "Pork Store," as Italians like to call their Butcher Shop. There's nothing like the human touch to ask for and get the best and freshest cuts of meat. The butcher may even tell you how best to cook it. Don't be afraid to ask. I do when not sure.

For **chicken**, you can buy organic or a brand with a reputation. Again, if in doubt, ask the butcher behind the counter.

For **fish**, the packing date is most important, since fresh fish has such a short shelf life. If the fish isn't packaged, ask the person behind the counter when the fish was caught. There should be no "fishy" odor to fish. It should look clean and all one color. Unless it's frozen, cook the fish the same day or the next day that you buy it.

Always wash your hands before and after handling foods, especially meats and fish. Make sure the countertops are also clean before and after.

The bottom line is to use fresh vegetables and herbs and the freshest cuts of meat and fish whenever possible. For olive oil, always choose extra-virgin. All the recipes in this book use extra-virgin olive oil, even though they may say only olive oil.

**And then there's price**. You'll know the average price or sale price for foods by shopping and /or looking at food ads. Take advantage of sales as this usually means the product is abundant.

My cousin Luca making dinner in Italy

# Appetizers

# Baked Clams

Ingredients:

2 cans minced clams
¾ cups bread crumbs
5 tbs. finely chopped onion
2 tbsps. Parsley, chopped
Pinch of Italian seasoning
Clam or oyster shells (optional)

¼ cup olive oil
½ lemon
3 cloves garlic, minced
1 tsp oregano or thyme
Grated Parmesan cheese

Directions:
1. Sauté onions in oil until for 3 min. until soft. Add garlic and sauté for 30 sec.
2. Add bread crumbs, sauté 30 sec. Remove pan from heat.
3. Add clams, its juice and ½ squeezed lemon. Mix together with a fork.
4. Put a heaping tablespoon on each shell or baking cup. (Mixture should be more loose than thick.)
5. Sprinkle Parmesan Cheese on top and bake in 450 F degree oven for 15 min., until brown and bubbly. Makes about 15 baked clams.

# Calamari Salad

This is delicious any time of year, either as an appetizer or as an added complement to a meal. The longer you marinade it, the better it tastes. Serve on crackers or eat with a fork by itself.

Ingredients:
- 1 ½ lbs. squid
- 2 tbs. lemon juice
- 1 tbs. red wine vinegar
- 1/3 cup olive oil
- 1 large, garlic clove, minced
- ½ tsp. salt
- ¼ tsp. black pepper
- 1 red onion, slivered
- ½ cup pitted, halved black olives or capers
- 2 celery ribs cut in ¼ inch slices
- ½ cup chopped, parsley leaves

Directions:
1- Rinse squid and dry with paper toweling. Cut bodies in 1/3 inch rings. Cut tentacles in half lengthwise.
2- Fill a pot ¾ with water. Bring to a boil.
3- Add squid and cook only 40-60 seconds, just as they turn white. Overcooking hardens them.
4- Drain in a colander and quickly cool with ice to stop cooking.
5- Place in a bowl and add all other ingredients. Toss well. Store in a tight container for at least an hour. The longer the better.

# Fried Calamari

Calamari (squid) is everyone's favorite and quick and easy to make, but delicate in that you cook it only 1 minute or so.  Serves 6

Ingredients:
- 1 lb. clean squid (calamari)
- 2 tbs. fresh parsley, chopped
- 1 or more cups of vegetable oil
- 1 cup of tomato-basil sauce or marinara sauce
- 2 cups flour
- salt, pepper to taste
- 1 lemon cut in wedges

Directions:
1. Cut squid tentacles and bodies into ½ inch rings.
2. Mix flour, parsley, salt and pepper in a large bowl.  Coat the squid with the flour mixture.
3. Heat oil about 2 inches deep in a large fry-pan and add the floured squid to fry 1 min., until pale golden.  With tongs or fork, transfer calamari to plate lined with paper toweling to absorb excess oil.
4. Place on serving dish, with lemon wedges and a cup of tomato or marinara sauce in which to dip the calamari.

# Caponata Pugliese

Typically known as a Sicilian dish, different versions of caponata are made throughout Italy. My friend, Terry, whose family comes from Sicily, makes it Sicilian style and just as delicious.

## Ingredients:

- 1 seedless eggplant, diced
- 2 carrots, peeled and diced
- 2 stalks of celery, diced
- 1 onion, diced
- 1 tbsp. capers
- 1 tsp. oregano
- Salt to taste
- 1 zucchini, diced
- 1 red pepper, diced
- 3 plum tomatoes
- ¼ cup olive oil
- 1 tsp. mint, chopped
- 1 tbsp. balsamic vinegar
- Pepperoncino (optional)

## Directions:

1. Wash and dry the vegetables before dicing. Remove outside strings of celery stalks.
2. Heat oil in pan. Add all vegetables and sauté 5 min on medium, stirring a few times, until browned. Eggplants readily absorb the oil so add more oil if vegetables seem too dry. Remove from pan into a plate.
3. In the same pan, add the onions and brown 3-4 minutes, then tomatoes, and capers. Cook 5 more minutes. Now return cooked vegetables to pan and add spices except mint. Stir, cooking one or two minutes more.
4. Place in a container, blend in the vinegar, top with mint leaves cover and refrigerate before serving.

# Frittata

This can make a hearty lunch or even a meal, depending on the ingredients included.

Ingredients:
- ¼ cup oil
- 5 eggs
- Sliced zucchini
- Salt and pepper to taste,
- cheddar cheese
- ½ cup milk
- 3 tbs. chopped onion
- a handful of Parmesan cheese
- Anything else you wish to add, e.g., diced peppers, mushrooms, diced tomato, diced sausage, diced potatoes.

Directions:
1. In a large skillet, heat oil and add onions. Sautee for 4 min. on medium heat until golden.
2. Blend eggs and milk and whip with fork. Put aside.
3. Add other ingredients except cheese to onions and cook on low to medium heat stirring to brown and cook both sides. If adding potatoes or sausage, sauté those for 3-4 minutes before adding zucchini and peppers.
4. Add egg-milk mixture to cover all ingredients in pan.
5. Add cheddar and/or sprinkle Parmesan cheese over omelet stirring omelet from sides of skillet from time to time.
6. When omelet is almost done, place a flat dish or cover over the top, turn the skillet upside down so omelet goes on dish, then slide omelet back onto the skillet and cook about another 2 or 3 minutes until done.

# Tomato-Mozzarella Appetizer

Delicious to eat and lovely to look at and there's no cooking, just assembling. The grated cheese could be Parmegiano, Pecorino, or Romano.

Ingredients:
- 2-3 slicing tomatoes
- 1-2 balls of buffalo mozzarella
- Drops of olive oil
- 1 teaspoon basil flakes
- 1 tsp. grated cheese
- 1 tsp. oregano or thyme
- 12 crackers or 12 pieces of lettuce
- 1 basil leaf (optional)

Directions:
1. On a serving dish or tray, layer the crackers or cut pieces of cleaned, dry lettuce leaves.
2. On a wooden board, cut tomatoes in thin slices and place one over each cracker or lettuce piece.
3. Drizzle top of tomato with one or two drops of olive oil, sprinkle some cheese, basil flakes and oregano or thyme.
4. Thinly slice the mozzarella and place one slice over each tomato. Top with basil leaf.

# Zucchini Pie

This makes a nice lunch, appetizer or side, especially in summer when zucchini is abundant.

Ingredients:

3 cups thinly sliced zucchini rounds  
½ onion, finely chopped  
½ cup grated cheese  
Pinch of pepper  
¼ cup olive oil  

1 cup of flour  
2 tbs. minced parsley  
1 tsp. salt  
½ tsp. oregano or thyme  
3 eggs beaten  

Directions:

Mix all ingredients together and put in an 8 or 9 inch greased pan and bake 45 min. at 350 F degrees.

**Mount Vesuvius viewed from Sant'Agnello, Italy**

# Soups and Salads

# Chicken Soup for a winter day or any day

This can be made with raw chicken or the leftovers from a cooked chicken. I use the latter because it gives our family one or two meals from the cooked chicken and then, by using the leftovers, we don't waste any meat attached to the bones. Fresh spices are best. If you use raw chicken, cook a little longer to insure meat is cooked fully.

Ingredients:

- Leftover chicken
- 1 garlic clove, diced
- 2 or 3 fresh carrots, diced
- Fresh parsley
- 1 tbsp. olive oil
- 4 or more cups water
- 1 onion, sliced
- 1 or 2 potatoes
- Handful of string beans
- Handful of rice
- ¼ cup white wine
- dried beans (optional)
- Sprinkles of salt, garlic powder, basil flakes, paprika, sage, pepper, rosemary

Directions:

1. In a large pot, add the oil and brown the onion on medium for 3-4 min. Lower flame and add garlic and sauté 30 sec.
2. Add chicken leftovers, discarding yellow fat but not the brown gel which is protein. Add enough water to fill pot ¾ full. Now add rice, salt and spices desired.
3. Peel carrots and potatoes, dice and add into pot. Remove ends from string beans if fresh, rinse and add to pot. Bring to a boil.
4. Add wine and simmer for 10-15 minutes. Soup is now ready to serve.
5. If adding the dried beans, rinse them and add them to pot before step 3. Bring to a boil and simmer for 1 hour. Then continue with steps 3 and 4 before serving.
6. *Bonus: When cool, freeze any leftover soup in serving sizes, label and date.*
   *When ready to use them, pull the container out of the freezer, turn upside down closed and run hot water from the sink on the container. Within a few seconds, the contents loosen from the container. Place frozen soup in pot and heat on high or medium high. Soup will defrost in about 10 min. ready to eat.*

# Minestrone

This is a traditional and hearty soup for Italians because it has their staple Mediterranean diet foods of tomatoes, beans and vegetables. You can substitute frozen peas and carrots for the fresh ones and canned beans for the dry ones you'd have to cook yourself. You can also use vegetable broth instead of chicken broth. The wine is my own take on the pasta.

## Ingredients:

- 1 large onion, chopped
- 2-3 ribs celery, chopped
- 2 fresh carrots, diced
- 1 cup cooked red beans
- ½ cup corn
- ½ tsp. oregano or thyme
- 6 cups chicken broth
- 1 tbsp. parsley, chopped
- 3 cloves garlic, minced
- 4 tomatoes, diced (or 1 can)
- 1-2 zucchini, cut in pieces
- 1 cup cooked white beans
- ½ tsp. dried basil
- ¼ cup of ditalini or elbow pasta
- ¼ cup of wine, red or white
- Parmesan cheese (optional)

## Directions:

1. Heat the oil in a large pot and brown for 3-5 min. on medium. Add garlic and everything else except the zucchini, wine and pasta. Bring to a boil and simmer for 15 min.
2. Meanwhile slice zucchini in rounds ¼ in. thick and cut each in half or in fours. After 15 min. of pot simmering, add zucchini pieces, wine and pasta and bring to a boil. Simmer 5 min. more until pasta is tender. Add more broth or water if too thick. Sprinkle with Parmesan cheese or eat as is. Delicious either way.

# Pasta e Fagioli

Again, this is the poor man's soup from Italy, but it is very healthy and delicious. Remember, you can add, subtract or substitute ingredients according to your tastes and what you have at home. For example, substitute 2 tbsp. tomato paste for tomatoes.

Ingredients:

¼ lbs. pancetta, bacon or pork
1 onion, finely chopped
1 celery rib, finely chopped
1 cup fresh plum tomatoes, diced
2 tbsp. Italian parsley, chopped
1 tsp. rosemary
Fresh basil leaves (optional)
1 tsp. sage
salt and pepper to taste
2 cans of kidney or cannellini beans
Grated Parmesan or Romano cheese (optional)

2 tbsp. olive oil
1 carrot, finely chopped
3 cloves garlic, chopped
2 cups chicken stock
2 cups water
1 tsp. basil
1 tsp. thyme or oregano
1 bay leaf
1 cup ditalini pasta

Directions:
1. Heat oil for 1 min on medium in large pot. Add onions and brown 2 min.
2. Add garlic, pancetta, herbs, carrots and celery. Stir and heat for 1 min.
3. Add tomatoes, chicken stock and remaining ingredients, except pasta.
4. Cover, bring to a boil and simmer for 15 min.
5. Add pasta and simmer for another 5-6 minutes, until tender. Serve into bowls.
6. Sprinkle with grated cheese and eat as is or with Italian bread.

# Green Salad

Italians love salad. They eat it at the end of the meal because, they say, it helps digest the food. In our family, we always eat it last. For me, the required parts are the lettuce, cucumber, tomato, salt, olive oil and vinegar. I use the optional ingredients when I have them, but the salad is delicious with or without them. When I dress the salad, I don't measure. I just pour the right amount with my hand and eyes. You can always adjust the amounts by using the taste test. For salad lighter on the digestive system, some Italians (Sicilians, especially) squeeze a lemon over the salad instead of using vinegar.

Ingredients:
- 1 head of Romaine or mixed leaves
- ½ peeled cucumber
- 1-2 tbs. balsamic or wine vinegar
- A handful of chives (optional)
- A handful of arugula (optional)
- ¼ cup olive oil
- 1 tomato, sliced
- ¼ tsp. salt
- fresh basil
- Pepper (optional)

Directions:
1. Wash lettuce leaves (if not pre-washed) by running under cold water and place in a salad bowl. Drain excess water by tipping bowl, holding salad in with your hand.
2. Break leaves into bite-size pieces with hands. Cover with paper toweling and tip bowl (your hand over toweling) to absorb and drain remaining water. Dry further, if needed.
3. Add remaining ingredients.
4. Toss and enjoy at the end, with or at the beginning of your meal, as you prefer.

# Fresh Tomato Salad

On a hot summer day, there's nothing like a salad of fresh tomatoes, especially homegrown, to stimulate your palate and bring the flavors of Italy directly into your mouth. And it's so easy to make!

Ingredients:
- 2 or more tomatoes
- Sprinkle of oregano and/or basil
- Drizzle of olive oil
- Sprinkle of salt

Directions:
1. Clean tomatoes under running water and cut in pieces.
2. Add spices. Drizzle with olive oil and stir. Delicious!

# Italian Potato Salad

This is great on a hot day, low in calories and rich in nutrients and flavor. You can increase or decrease the ingredient amounts to make for 2 or 20.

Ingredients:
- 6-8 potatoes
- 1 tsp. salt
- 1tsp. oregano or thyme
- ½ cup olive oil
- 1 tsp basil

Directions:
1. Boil unpeeled whole potatoes in water for 20 min., until tender when pricked with fork. Or peel and cut potatoes in cubes and boil for 5-7 min. until tender.
2. Drain water. (If potatoes are whole and need to be peeled, run potatoes under cold water and skin is easier to peel. Cut potatoes in bite-size cubes.) Place cut potatoes in serving bowl. Add salt, spices and drizzle with olive oil and toss to blend ingredients. Cool in refrigerator or serve at room temperature.

Garden at Museo di Valentino, Castellaneta, Italy, with permission

# Three Bean Salads

This recipe is from another Italian friend named Terry, whose family comes from Ancona, Italy. She is a wonderful cook herself and has taught me more than a few things about cooking and baking. This salad is so easy to make and perfect in summer.

Ingredients:
- 2 cans cut green beans
- 1 can of any other bean desired
- ½ cup sweet green pepper, chopped
- ½ cup vinegar
- 2 tbsp. sugar
- 1 clove dry mustard
- 1 can kidney beans
- ½ cup chopped onion
- ½ cup chopped celery
- ¼ cup canola oil
- ½ tsp. dry mustard

Directions:
1. In a bowl, combine all beans, onion, celery and sweet pepper.
2. In another bowl combine vinegar, oil dry mustard and garlic. Mix well and pour over vegetables and gently mix. Cover and chill for 4-24 hours, stirring from time to time.

# Pasta

# Fettuccini or Other Fresh Long Pasta

For any homemade pasta, it's best to have a pasta machine for shaping it thin and even. Sprinkle some flour through opening of pasta machine and pass a small piece of dough that you can discard. Then pass dough as in step 7.

Ingredients:
- 4 cups flour
- 1 tbs. olive oil
- 1 tbsp. buttermilk (optional)
- 4 eggs
- pinch of salt

Directions:
1. Place flour on a clean wooden board or granite countertop.
2. Make a well in center and add eggs, oil, salt and buttermilk.
3. Mix and knead for 5 min. until smooth.
4. Cover with cotton cloth to rest for 15 min.
5. Pull a small section of dough and shape into a log 7 in. long. Flatten with your hands or rolling pin.
6. Put flattened dough through pasta machine, first on 1, then 3, then 5.
7. Lay fettuccini on a floured surface and repeat steps 5 to 7 for rest of dough.
8. Boil pasta for about 2-3 minutes only, al dente. Fresh past gets done quickly.

# Gnocchi

This is my mother's recipe and another festive meal for a large gathering, serving 20.

## Ingredients:

10 large potatoes (5lbs.)   10 cups flour
6 eggs, beaten   ½ cup chopped parsley
2 tbsp. chopped basil

## Directions:

1. Boil potatoes whole 15-20 min. until tender. Cool under running cold water and peel off skins. Then mash potatoes by hand.
2. Combine 8 cups of flour with potatoes and place on a floured wooden board or granite surface. Make a well in the center and add eggs, parsley and basil. Blend well with hands until it reaches consistency of dough. Add more flour if sticky or another egg if too dry.
3. Cut off a piece and shape into a thin log about 12 in. long and ½ in. diameter. Cut log into ¾ inch pieces.
4. Flour a cheese grater and, with thumb, press each piece against grater. Flick it and let it roll onto floured cookie sheet. Pieces look like cavatelli pasta.
5. Repeat steps 4 and 5 with rest of dough.
6. Boil water in a very large pot. Add salt and 1 tsp. oil so pasta does not stick.
7. Add gnocchi and cook until they rise (about 2 min.), stirring gently with wooden spoon. Ladle out gnocchi with a slotted spoon. If pot is not big enough for all the gnocchi, cook gnocchi in two or three batches in the same water, always returning water to a boil once each batch is removed.
8. Place some red sauce on the bottom of a serving bowl, then, add gnocchi. Add more red sauce on top and sprinkle with chopped basil. Serve with grated Pecorino, Romano or Parmegiano cheese. Or mix gnocchi with pesto sauce and serve. Delicious, either way.

*Tip: You can freeze uncooked gnocchi by leaving them on a cookie sheet in freezer until firm and then placing them in a freezer bag.*

# Lasagna

Lasagna is, perhaps, the queen of pasta. It can be prepared in advance and makes a festive presentation.

Ingredients:
  I package of lasagna pasta     3 cups or more tomato sauce
  1 lbs. mozzarella, sliced      2 lbs. Ricotta cheese
  Grated Parmesan or Romano cheese

Directions:
1. Bring a large pot of salted water to boil and drop in lasagna pasta individually. When softened by the water, gently stir so they don't stick together. Cook about 7 min.
2. Drain pasta onto a colander and layer a few of the noodles over the sides of the pot. You can add some cold water to cool it and keep it from sticking.
3. Line a large baking pan with tomato sauce. Sprinkle with Parmesan or Romano cheese. Layer each lasagna noodle to lay flat in pan. Spread spoonsful of ricotta over the noodles, add more sauce and grated cheese. Now add mozzarella slices.
4. Layer more lasagna noodles on top and repeat step 3, continuing to layer until all the lasagna noodles are used up. Usually 3 or 4 layers are attained. Bake in a 375 F for degree oven 15-20 min., until sides bubble.
5. To keep lasagna intact when serving, cut through into lasagna with a knife to create serving sizes before lifting them with spatula.

# Linguine with Mussels and Clams Marinara or in White Sauce

Ingredients:

Bag of fresh, live Mussels
2-3 large cloves garlic
½ cup dry white wine
1 tsp sage
1 tsp basil flakes or fresh basil
¼ cup olive oil
1 stalk celery cut up
2 tbsp. chopped parsley
1 tsp rosemary flakes
1 tsp oregano or thyme
1 can diced tomatoes (omit tomatoes for white sauce)
Salt, pepper to taste
pepperoncino, optional

Directions:
1. Scrub muscles with hands or brush to remove sand. DISCARD ANY OPENED MUSCLES!
2. Heat oil in large pan and add all ingredients except mussels. Sauté for 5 min.
3. Add clean, CLOSED mussels, cover and cook 5-7 min., until mussels open.
4. Fill pot with ¾ salted water and bring to a boil.
5. Add pasta separately, cook 5-7 min., al dente, drain but keep some of salted pasta water.
6. Mix pasta and mussels in a bowl. If too dry, add some pasta water and olive oil. Sprinkle with some chopped parsley and serve.

# Linguine alla Puttanesca

Ingredients:

    2 cans of anchovies in oil      1 onion minced
    2 cloves garlic, minced      2 tbsp. chopped parsley
    ½ cup black olives      salt, hot pepper to taste
    5-8 fresh plum tomatoes or a 12 oz. can crushed tomatoes
    ¼ cup olive oil

Directions:

1. Heat oil in a fry-pan and sauté onions for 3-5 min. Add garlic, then, anchovies and cook 2 min. longer.
2. Add tomatoes, olives parsley, salt and pepper and simmer 15 min.
3. Meanwhile, boil salted water in a large pot, then, add pasta. Cook *al dente*, 7 min. or 2-3 min. if pasta is fresh.
4. Drain pasta through a colander and place in a serving dish.
5. Pour anchovies-tomato mixture over pasta, stir and serve.

# Orecchiette

This is the traditional pasta for all festive occasions in my hometown of Castellaneta and throughout all of Puglia. The word means little ears, which is the shape of the pasta.

Ingredients:
    3 cups flour                                  2 eggs
    Lukewarm water

Directions:
1. Place flour on kneading surface. Make a well. Add 2 eggs and work into flour. Add a little water and work into flour, continuing to add more water until the consistency becomes dough that is not sticky but workable.
2. Pinch pieces of dough off and roll into logs, breadstick size.
3. With a knife, cut into ¼ in. pieces, roll each cut piece with the edge of the knife to flatten it. Sides curl somewhat. With thumb, turn each piece inside out and lay on a flowered board or cookie tin until all the dough is used up.
4. For cooking, boil enough water in a large pot, add salt, then the orecchiette and bring back to a boil. Cook al dente, 2 or 3 min. Drain and serve with tomato sauce and Pecorino-Romano cheese sprinkled on top. Delicious!

*In the next photos, you'll find my cousin Peppino helping his wife Maria as she makes orecchiette with a knife and her thumb faster than one can imagine. I have to admit that I am not as fast as she is.*

# Pasta with Cauliflower or Broccoli

Ingredients:
- 1 lb. pasta
- 1/3 cup olive oil
- 1 tsp salt
- 1-2 large cloves garlic
- 1 large stalk cauliflower or broccoli

Directions:
1. Fill a large pot ¾ with salted water and bring to a boil.
2. Wash cauliflower or broccoli. Cut off hard part of stem. Cut in small pieces.
3. Place pasta in boiling salted water and cook for 4 min. Add cauliflower or broccoli and cook until both pasta and vegetables are *al dente*, about 4 min. more. Drain pasta in a colander but keep some of the pasta water.
4. In another large pan, add olive oil to cover the bottom and heat. Cut up one or two large cloves of garlic and sauté on medium heat for 30 sec., until golden.
5. Place pasta and vegetables in pan with olive oil and toss. If pasta is too dry, add some of the pasta water and toss. Sprinkle with pepper and/or cheese as desired.

**A Cheese Shop in Milan**

# Spaghetti Carbonara

Again, this is my mother's recipe, about 15-20 servings, which shows that she made this when the whole family got together. The ingredients can be divided into smaller amounts to suit the number of servings needed. It is a very festive meal.

## Ingredients:

- 1 lbs. pancetta, diced
- 2 bunches parsley finely chopped
- 3 pounds of pasta
- 8 ounces of parmesan cheese
- 2 sticks of butter
- 10 garlic cloves, minced
- ¼ cup of olive oil
- 16 eggs
- 1 pint of heavy cream
- Salt and black pepper

## Directions:

1. Heat the olive oil in a fry pan. Add garlic and pancetta and sauté for 2-3 minutes. Stir in butter and parsley. Cover and set aside.
2. Boil salted water in large pot. Add pasta and 1 teaspoon of oil so pasta does not stick together. Boil 7 min., *al dente*.
3. In the meantime, beat eggs in a bowl and sprinkle with black pepper and set aside.
4. Drain pasta and return it to the pot it boiled in. Keep pot on low on top of stove. Mix in egg mixture and pancetta mixture. Stir into pasta. Add heavy cream and Parmesan cheese. Continue stirring with two big forks. Place in a large bowl and serve.

My mother who loved to cook

# Seafood - Pesce

**Fishing Boats in Bay of Sorrento**

# Flounder, Tilapia, Swordfish, Sole Fillets
# Grilled, Broiled or Baked

Ingredients:

    2 fish fillets  
    2 or 3 tablespoons of olive oil  
    ½ tsp. black pepper  
    ½ tsp. paprika  
    ¼ cup white wine.  

    1 clove of garlic, minced  
    ½ tsp. salt.  
    ½ tsp. garlic powder  
    ½ tsp. dried basil flakes  
    Lemon zest (lemon peel)

Directions:

1. Place all ingredients, except fish, in a bowl or cup. Mix well and pour over fish. Or administer each ingredient over fillets separately.
2. Flip fillets to marinade both sides. Marinade for 1 min. or a few hours.
3. Bake for about 5 minutes on each side at 400 degrees until tender. Or, grill or bake about 3 min. on each side until tender.

The Scent of Italian Cooking

# Salmon Fillets

## Ingredients

2 salmon fillets  
2 or 3 tablespoons of olive oil  
½ tsp. black pepper  
½ tsp. paprika  
¼ cup white wine.  
1 clove of garlic, minced  
½ tsp. salt.  
½ tsp. garlic powder  
½ tsp. dried basil flakes  
1 tbs. mustard (optional)  
Lemon zest (thin scrapings of lemon peel)

## Directions:

1. Place all ingredients, except salmon, in a bowl or cup. Mix well and pour over salmon. Or administer each ingredient over fillets separately.
2. Bake for about 10 to 15 minutes in a 400 degree oven or grill or broil for about 5 minutes on high.

Salmon is also good with just salt, pepper, olive oil, lemon juice and wine over it and cooked the same way.

# Lobster

Lobsters should always be bought alive. Once home, never put them in water or on ice. Simply put them in the refrigerator with the bag open so they can breathe. Cook that day or the next. Do not remove rubber band around their claws until ready to cook. I learned how to cook, serve and eat lobster from a friend who came from Maine. Though it will be the main entre of the meal, I like to eat it first, like an appetizer, as it is takes time to remove the meat from all the shell. A shrimp or lobster fork or pick is helpful in getting it all out. Many people eat the roe (red or green mass in body of lobster) and suck out all the meat in the tentacles. Serve with a chilled bottle of Chardonnay and you are set. After I've relished all the lobster, I'm ready to eat the sides.

Ingredients:
    Lobsters (1 per person)    ¼ stick butter per person
    Lemon (optional)    Garlic powder (optional)

Directions:
1. In a pot large enough to fit lobsters, fill ¾ full with water. Cover and bring to a boil. Add lobsters one at a time with the rubber band on or off, being careful to grab lobster by its body either with your fingers or with tongs.
2. Cover and bring to a boil. Boil for 10 min. for 1 ½ lbs., 12-15 min. for larger lobsters, until they turn orange.
3. Drain some or all the water. With tongs, pull lobster out and place on a plate.
4. With a strong pair of scissors, cut anterior part (head) off, then turn lobster on its back and make an incision on soft membrane of tail end up.
5. With nut crackers (or hammer, as my friend from Maine does), crack claws.
6. Pick up lobster to drain excess water and place on a serving dish to eat or keep warm in a warm oven. Repeat steps 4 and 5 with other lobsters.
7. Melt butter in individual dishes or cups in micro for 30 sec. Serve and eat by dipping lobster pieces in butter.

# Mahi-Mahi

Hawaiian fish that has become popular on the mainland.

## Ingredients:

2 Mahi Mahi fillets
2 or 3 tablespoons of olive oil
½ tsp. black pepper
½ tsp. paprika
¼ cup white wine.
Macadamia nuts, chopped (optional)

1 clove of garlic, minced
½ tsp. salt.
½ tsp. garlic powder
½ tsp. dried basil flakes
Lemon zest (lemon peel)

## Directions:

1. Place all ingredients, except fish, in a bowl or cup. Mix well and pour over fish. Or administer each ingredient over fillets separately. Turn fillets to marinade both sides. Marinade for 1 min. or a few hours.
2. Barbeque for about 5 minutes on each side at 400 degrees until tender.
3. Sprinkle with Macadamia nuts and serve.

# Shrimp with Curried Rice and Vegetables

A quick and easy recipe that's delicious every time. Salad and bread are nice additions.

Ingredients:
- 1 cup of rice
- 1 lb. clean deveined shrimp
- 1 cup stir-fries (veg. medley)
- 1 large onion sliced
- 1 small, garlic clove, minced
- 1/3 cup extra virgin olive oil
- 2 tsps. Curry
- ¼ cup of dry white wine
- ½ tsp. each of salt, garlic powder, paprika, basil flakes, rosemary, black pepper to taste

Directions:
1. Prepare rice according to package directions. Let stand when done.
2. Heat olive oil in a skillet. Add onions, sauté for 5 min.
3. Add garlic, sauté 1 min. Add veg., all spices except curry, wine. Cover 5 min. Stir.
4. Add cleaned shrimp to vegetable mixture. Sprinkle more olive oil, if needed, and add the wine. Sauté 1 or 2 min., turning shrimp once, until shrimp lose their off-white color and become orange.
5. Add curry to rice. Sprinkle with some garlic powder, paprika, basil flakes and some olive oil. Stir with a fork and mound rice in a large serving dish. With a large spoon, top rice with shrimp-vegetable combination and its juices. Or serve the rice and shrimp-vegetable combo separately in individual plates.

# Shrimp with Pasta and Vegetables

Ingredients:

    1 lb. clean deveined shrimp      ½ lb. pasta
    1 small onion sliced      1 garlic clove, minced
    ½ cup extra virgin olive oil      ¼ cup of dry white wine
    1 tsp. garlic powder      ½ tsp. paprika
    1 tsp. basil flakes      1 tsp. rosemary
    ½ tsp. black pepper      salt to taste
    1 package or about 1 cup of vegetables
(String beans, broccoli, sliced zucchini, vegetables to your liking.)

Directions:

1. Fill a pot ¾ with salted water and bring to a boil. Add pasta, cook al dente 5-7 min., stirring and drain.
2. While water and pasta boil, heat olive oil in a skillet. Add onions, sauté for 5 min.
3. Add garlic, sauté 1 min. Add veg., spices, wine. Cover, simmer 5 min., and stir.
4. Remove the vegetables (not onions) from the pan and put them in covered dish.
5. Add cleaned shrimp in the pan. Sprinkle more olive oil and wine. Sauté 1 or 2 min., turning shrimp once, until shrimp lose their off-white color and become orange.
6. Add the pasta to the shrimp and stir all together so the pasta is covered with the sauce. Mix in vegetables or serve them on side in a large dish. It is delicious.

# Barbecued Shrimp
(Delicious as a dinner or appetizer)

Ingredients:
- 1 lb. raw shrimp, cleaned and deveined
- 1 small, garlic clove, minced
- ½ cup olive oil
- ¼ cup of dry white wine
- ½ tsp. garlic powder,
- ½ tsp. paprika
- ½ tsp. basil flakes
- ½ tsp. rosemary
- ½ tsp. black pepper
- 1 tsp. finely chopped parsley
- Salt to taste

Directions:
1. Peel off hard, outer shell of shrimp. Rinse and dry the shrimp.
2. Cut off a large enough strip of aluminum foil and shape into a bowl.
3. Place shrimp in bowl and add all ingredients. Stir.
4. Place on barbecue with top open for 3-4 min. until shrimp is slightly cooked.
5. Seal top to keep juices and flavors in. Eat as an appetizer or place over cooked pasta or rice for a delicious meal.

# Flounder, Tilapia, Sole Fillets, Breaded

Ingredients:
- 2 fillets
- 1 egg
- 1/4 cup seasoned bread crumbs
- 1 tbsp. milk
- ¼ cup olive oil
- salt to taste

Directions:
1. Add milk to egg and beat together with a fork.
2. Coat fillets in egg batter, then with bread crumbs.
3. Heat oil in fry pan on medium.
4. When oil sizzles, add fillets and brown about 2 min. each side.
5. When done, place in dish with paper toweling to absorb excess oil.

# Shrimp Scampi

Delicious to eat and it makes a great presentation. Increase or decrease the amount of chopped garlic according to your taste.

Ingredients:

    20 raw jumbo shrimp      3-4 cloves garlic
    ¼ tsp. garlic powder      ¼ tsp. paprika
    ¼ tsp. basil flakes      ½ stick butter
    ¼ cup olive oil

Directions:

1. Remove shells and vein from shrimp. Rinse under water and drain in a colander. Dry with paper toweling.
2. Finely chop garlic. In a cup with a spout, add all ingredients except the shrimp and place in microwave to heat for 30 sec.
3. In a large, oiled cookie sheet or baking pan, arrange shrimp to lie individually. Sprinkle with some olive oil.
4. Broil for 3-4 minutes, until they turn orange.
5. Turn each shrimp to other side and pour heated liquid from micro over each shrimp. Broil another 1-3 min, until shrimp is done.
6. Place shrimp, with juices and garlic over cooked rice and serve.

# MEAT - CARNE

# Chicken Cacciatore

The word "cacciatore" means "hunter" in Italian. Chicken cacciatore is an easy, traditional meal hunters ate, which is the chicken they caught and fresh herbs and vegetables grown from their garden.

Ingredients:

- Chicken cut up in parts
- 1 tsp black pepper
- 3 tbsp. olive oil
- 1 bell pepper, chopped
- 3/4 cup dry white wine
- 28 oz. can diced tomatoes
- ½ tsp. dried oregano leaves
- 1 tsp salt
- 1/2 cup flour
- 1 onion, chopped
- 3 garlic cloves, chopped
- 3 tbsp. drained capers
- ¾ cup chicken broth
- 1/4 cup basil leaves

Directions:

1. Sprinkle the chicken pieces with 1 teaspoon of each salt and pepper. Dredge the chicken pieces in the flour to coat lightly.
2. In a large heavy sauté pan, heat the oil over a medium-high heat.
3. Add the chicken pieces to the pan and sauté just until brown, about 5 minutes per side. If all the chicken does not fit in the pan, sauté it in 2 batches.
4. Transfer the chicken to a plate to keep warm and set aside.
5. To the same pan, add the bell pepper, onion and garlic and sauté over medium heat until the onion is tender, about 5 minutes. Season with salt and pepper.
6. Add the wine. Simmer until reduced by half, 3-5 min.
7. Add tomatoes with their juice, broth, capers and oregano.
8. Return the chicken pieces to the pan and turn them to coat in the sauce. Bring sauce to a simmer. Continue simmering over medium-low heat until the chicken is just cooked through, about 15 min. for the breast pieces, and 20 minutes for the thighs.
9. Using tongs, transfer the chicken to a platter. If necessary, boil the sauce until it thickens slightly, about 3 minutes. Spoon off any excess fat from atop the sauce. Spoon the sauce over the chicken. Sprinkle with the basil and serve.

# Chicken in the Oven (Baked)

This is one of the easiest meals to make as it practically cooks itself, can feed 4-6 people and it has the most delicious flavor from the protein that develops in cooking. The meal is perfect on a winter day or a cool summer day as it warms up the house and your stomach. Any leftovers make great sandwiches for lunch. I often cook a whole chicken and use it just for sandwiches. Much better than cold cuts or chicken you buy already cooked. When you refrigerate the chicken, the yellow fat hardens and can be scooped out with a knife or spoon. The brown protein also hardens and separates from the fat. Pour some of it over the cut chicken slices or pieces and microwave for a most delicious flavor. It's healthy. Waste nothing. After you've removed most of the meat from the chicken, use the bones to make the most delicious homemade chicken soup. I show you how easy that is in the recipe under Soups. Be sure to wash hands, utensils, sink and other surfaces with hot sudsy water after dealing with meats, especially chicken.

Ingredients:
- 1 whole chicken
- ½ tsp. paprika
- ½ tsp. salt
- 1 small onion, sliced
- ½ tsp. garlic powder

Directions:
1. Set oven temperature to 450 degrees F.
2. Remove and discard any loose parts inside chicken cavity. Cut off end appendage and any visible fat (looks yellow) near end cavity.
3. Rinse inside and outside of chicken, drain and place in large roasting pan.
4. Sprinkle top half of chicken with half of paprika, garlic powder and salt.
5. Turn chicken to other side and repeat step 4.
6. Add sliced onions in pan. Cover. Place pan in oven. Set timer 30 min.
7. After 30 min., turn chicken to other side, cover and cook 30 min. more.
8. Serve on platter with some of its juices and onions whole or cut into pieces.

Whole Chicken in the Oven

Barbecued Chicken

# Barbecued Chicken

My mother gave me this recipe. I think of her every time I make it. This chicken recipe can also be baked in the oven, where you'd bake it at 400 degrees for 15-20 min. on each side.

Ingredients:
- Whole chicken cut in pieces
- ½ tsp. paprika
- ½ tsp. basil flakes and/or oregano
- ¼ cup lemon juice
- 1 tsp. salt
- ½ tsp. garlic powder
- ½ tsp. pepper
- ¼ cup white wine

Directions:
1. Remove skin from cut pieces by pulling and cutting with a knife.
2. Place pieces in large pan where they lie individually and sprinkle salt and spices and half of lemon juice over each piece.
3. With a fork, turn each piece to its other side and repeat step 2.
4. Cover with plastic wrap or aluminum foil and marinate from 5 min. - 2 days.
5. Place each piece on hot barbecue and grill on medium-low for 10 min.
6. Turn pieces over and grill for 10 min. more. Breast meat cooks quicker than dark.
7. Put leftover marinade juice in a cup and microwave until it boils, about 1 minute.
8. Place cooked chicken in a serving dish and pour juice over each piece.

# Chicken in the Micro

Ingredients:
- Whole chicken cut in pieces
- ½ tsp. paprika
- ½ tsp. basil flakes and/or oregano
- ¼ cup lemon juice
- 1 tsp. salt
- ½ tsp. garlic powder
- ½ tsp. pepper
- ¼ cup white wine

Directions:
1. Remove skin from cut pieces by pulling and cutting with a knife.
2. Place pieces in large dish or glass pan where they lie individually and sprinkle salt and spices and half of lemon juice over each piece.
3. Put dish or pan in micro, cover with wax paper or protective dish and microwave on high for 10 min.
4. Take dish out of micro and turn chicken pieces over. Repeat steps 2 and 3, cover and microwave on high for 10 more min.

# Chicken and Potatoes

You can always substitute dry spices if you don't have the fresh ones. Use wing tips to make chicken stock by placing in 3 cups of water and adding garlic powder, pepper, salt and half onion, boiling low for 20 min. Serves 4-6

Ingredients:

- 1 chicken, cut up
- 12-15 small red potatoes
- Sprig of oregano
- ½ cup chicken stock
- 2 carrots cut lengthwise, 3 in. long
- Sage and/or bay leaf
- ¼ cup olive oil
- Sprig of rosemary
- fennel leaves
- 1 small onion, sliced
- 2 celery stalks, cut up
- salt, pepper to taste

Directions:

1. Heat olive oil in pan and sauté chicken legs and thighs with skin side down. After 3-4 min, turn legs and thighs to other side. Now add white meat pieces, which cook faster. Turn to other side.
2. When all sides are brown, add the spices. Cover and let cook for 3-4 min. Remove from pan and cover to stay warm.
3. Cut potatoes in half and place in pan cut side down. Add onions to brown together with potatoes for 3-4 min. Place chicken on top of potatoes and onions. Add chicken stock, cover and let simmer for 10-15 min. to reduce liquid, but keep chicken and vegetables moist.

# Chicken or Veal Cutlet Parmesan

Ingredients:

    6-8 cutlets sliced thin              2 cups tomato sauce
    ½ to 1 cup seasoned bread crumbs  1 lbs. mozzarella, sliced
    ½ cup extra virgin olive oil         ¼ cup of dry white wine
    2 eggs                                   ¼ cup milk
    Grated Parmesan or Romano cheese  salt, seasonings to taste.

Directions:

1. Combine eggs and milk and whip with a fork. Sprinkle and blend in salt, garlic powder, pepper or other desired seasonings.
2. Place a layer of bread crumbs on a flat plate. Take one cutlet at a time and coat both sides with bread crumbs, then dip in the egg mixture and coat both sides and again in the bread crumbs coating both sides.
3. Warm oil in fry pan for 2 min on medium heat until it sizzles when a drop of water is sprinkled over it. Place enough cutlets to fill pan, leaving some room for turning. Brown for 3 or 4 min. on one side, then with a spatula, flip cutlets to brown on the other side. Remove when done and place in a dish lined with paper toweling to absorb excess oil. Repeat until all cutlets are used up.
4. Line a large baking pan with tomato sauce. **Sprinkle with Parmesan or Romano cheese.** Now layer cutlets to fit in pan. Add more sauce over each cutlet and sprinkle again with grated cheese.
5. Cover each cutlet with a slice of mozzarella and bake in a 400 F degree oven for 15 minutes, until sauce on pan sides bubbles and mozzarella melts.

# Pork Chops with French Fries

Ingredients:

2 or more center cut pork chops  1 egg
¼ to ½ cup seasoned bread crumbs  ¼ cup milk
2-4 potatoes  ¼ cup olive oil
Sprinkles of garlic powder, paprika, basil flakes, salt/ pepper

Directions:
1. Sprinkle some olive oil in a large baking pan and spread with fingers.
2. In a bowl, combine egg, milk and spices. Whip together.
3. Place bread crumbs in a flat dish and smooth evenly.
4. Soak both sides of each chop in egg mixture, then coat with bread crumbs.
5. Repeat step 4 as this will give a nice crust to chops and keep moisture in.
6. Place chops in baking pan.
7. Peel and cut potatoes lengthwise and arrange flat next to chops, using the rest of the pan surface. Sprinkle spices and olive oil on potatoes and chops. Bake in a 375 F degree oven for 15 min., until top of chops are golden.
8. With a spatula, turn chops and potatoes over to other side. Bake about 15 min. longer until golden. Serve with home-made apple sauce, vegetables and salad.

Uncooked Pork Chops and Potatoes

**Cooked Pork Chops and Potatoes**

# Lamb Chops Barbecued or Broiled

Ingredients:
- 4 loin lamb chops
- 1 clove garlic
- Basil flakes
- Paprika
- Lemon zest
- ¼ cup white wine
- rosemary
- garlic powder
- salt
- mint jelly, optional

Directions:
1. Place lamb chops in a dish. Insert a pointed knife into each chop 1 in. deep and make 3 separate holes.
2. Cut garlic in thin strips and place 1 strip in each hole. Place I or 2 rosemary sticks in the same hole.
3. Marinade by sprinkling with olive oil, salt, lemon zest, wine and spices.
4. Turn each chop over and repeat steps 1, 2 and 3.
5. Barbecue or Broil 3-4 min. on high. Turn chops and cook another 3-4 minute. Meat is delicious rare or medium.
6. In the meantime, place dish with marinade over warm barbecue or heat in microwave for 30 seconds. When chops are done, return them to the dish with marinade and serve with mint jelly if desired. Curried rice, French fries or pasta with pesto make a great accompaniment.

# Turkey with Dressing

A must for Thanksgiving Day. This recipe is from my mother-in-law who taught me how to cook many "American" type foods. My children grew up on her turkey dressing and love it over any other.

## Ingredients:

Large turkey (20-24lbs.)
1 large, garlic clove chopped fine
1 stick butter
2 lbs. hearty white bread (Arnold)
1 cup home-made apple sauce
3 tbs. flour

1 onion, chopped fine
2 tbs. parsley chopped
1tsp. basil flakes
Turkey stock
2 large eggs
water

## Directions:

1. **Prepare apple sauce in advance:** peel about 10 Red Delicious apples. Slice them and drop them in a large pot. Sprinkle them with cinnamon (about 1 tbs.), then add ½ cup of water, cover and cook on medium for 20-30 minutes until slices are soft. Stir with a fork to make a rough mixture.
2. Take turkey out of its wrapper and plan on following cooking instructions for that size turkey. Usually 15 min. per lb. at 325 degrees Fahrenheit.
3. **Prepare turkey stock:** take out neck, gizzard and liver out of turkey cavity. Discard the gizzard and liver. Rinse the neck and place it in a saucepot filled ¾ with water. Add a sprinkle of salt and garlic powder, cover and cook for about 15-20 min.
4. **Prepare stuffing:** place the stick of butter in a dish and melt or soften it in the micro (30 sec. on high).
5. Place a layer of bread slices across a large baking pan. Sprinkle the bread with minced onion, garlic, parsley and basil. Add butter and several spoonsful of the liquid from the pot with the neck. Add some of the cooked applesauce, and eggs. With a fork or fingers, mix all ingredients until well-blended.
6. Repeat layer of bread and applesauce until all is used up and mix ingredients again to create a smooth consistency.

7. Spoon dressing into neck and body cavities of turkey and bake the turkey breast side up at 325 degrees according to turkey package instructions.
8. After 2 hours, cover turkey with aluminum foil so it doesn't over-brown.
9. When turkey is done, let it stand for 15-20 minutes on a cutting board. Pour the turkey oils into a container and place in the freezer to cool and separate fat from juices. About 15-20 minutes.
10. Spoon out dressing from cavities, then, carve the turkey.
11. **Make gravy** by spooning out turkey fat from top of gravy cooled container. Place the lean gravy in a clean fry pan. Add 1 tbsp. flour to ½ cup water and, with a wisk, stir until smooth. Add to fry pan and continue stirring, repeating the process until gravy is the consistency of thin pancake syrup. **Pour some gravy onto dressing and mix.** Serve the rest at the table with the turkey.

# Osso Buco (Veal or Pork Shanks)

Literally, bone hole, a favorite dish of mine that I like to make for special occasions. The bone has meat (pork or veal) on the outside and bone marrow inside its hole, perfect for people who are anemic as red blood cells are manufactured in the bone marrow. It does require more time to prepare, but the flavor is worth the effort. One shank per person is usually enough. *Tip: If you do not have beef or chicken broth, substitute with ½ cup of water. If you do not have all the herbs, use what you have or substitute others for those mentioned, for example, no bay leaf or sage? Add thyme and basil, fresh or dry. No tomato paste? Add 2 or 3 sliced fresh tomatoes or a small can of whole, cut or crushed tomatoes.*

## Ingredients:

Veal or pork shanks
½ onion, chopped
2-3 carrots cut diagonally
¼ cup flour
½ - 1 cup white wine
1 sage leaf and 1 bay leaf
Salt and pepper to taste
¼ cup olive oil
2 stalks celery or fennel
2 tbsp. tomato paste
¼ tsp. or sprig rosemary
1 cup broth
Orange or lemon zest

## Directions:

1. Heat oil in casserole. Dust shanks with flour, add to casserole and brown both sides. Remove and keep warm.
2. In same casserole, sauté onions, carrots and celery or fennel for 5 min.
3. Add tomato paste, shanks, broth and half of white wine. Add salt, stir and cover.
4. Prepare a bundle of spices by putting together rosemary, bay and sage leaves, scrapings (zest) of outer skin of orange or lemon and any other spices of your choice and tie with string in all 4 directions so they stay confined. Add to mixture. Cover, simmer 1 hour, until meat on bone is tender when pierced with fork.
5. Remove bag of spices, mash vegetables with a fork or through a strainer or leave as is. Add the rest of the wine and simmer 5 more min.
6. Serve with rice, potatoes or pasta. Be sure to pour much of the juices over meat and over potato, rice or pasta.

# Veal Saltimbocca

Ingredients:

6 veal cutlets, thin-sliced (Scallopine) ½ cup flour
6 pieces of prosciutto, sliced thin    ½ tsp. garlic powder
6 pieces of provolone, thinly sliced   ½ tsp. white pepper
¼ cup olive oil                        ½ cup Marsala wine
1 tsp. corn starch                     Dash of salt
1 tbsp. butter

Directions:
1. Put flour, garlic powder, salt and pepper in a plastic bag and shake to blend.
2. Put veal in the bag, one slice at a time, to get coated with flour mixture.
3. Heat oil in a fry pan and sauté floured veal slices 1 min. on each side until golden.
4. Place slice of prosciutto and slice of provolone on each cutlet and remove from heat.
5. In another pan, melt butter. In a small bowl, mix cornstarch with 1 tsp. of water to make a paste. Add to butter. Now add white wine and simmer 3 min. Pour over cutlets in other pan and keep warm for a few min. before serving.

*Tip: For Veal Marsala, skip the provolone cheese and prosciutto and add sautéed mushrooms.*

# Tomato Sauce with Meatballs, Pork Ribs, Sausage

(Always best with fresh plum tomatoes)

## Ingredients:

2 lbs. lean chopped beef  
2 28oz. cans of plum tomatoes  
1 can of tomato paste  
6 cloves garlic, minced  
¼ cup olive oil  
2 lbs. country-style pork spare ribs  
6 sausages  
1 medium onion, minced  
½ cup parsley, minced  
2 eggs  
2 tsp. each of salt, pepper, rosemary, sage, basil  
½ cup parmesan or pecorino grated cheese  
4-5 slices of hearty white bread, moistened  

## Directions:

1. **Brown meats:** Heat olive oil in a large pot on medium heat. Place ribs and sausages to brown on one side, then the other. Remove and place on a plate.
2. **Prepare sauce:** Add ½ onions to pot (Pour extra oil if needed). Brown and stir for 3-5 min. Add garlic. Brown 30 sec.
3. Add tomatoes, paste and ½ of spices and stir. Fill tomato paste can with water and add to the pot, scraping any excess paste into the pot. Stir; add braised sausages and ribs, cover pot, bring to a boil. Now simmer for 1 hour.
4. **Prepare meatballs** by placing ground beef in a wide dish or casserole. Add rest of onion, garlic, cheese, eggs, parsley and other spices. Mix with a fork or your hands. Layer bread slices on top and moisten them by pouring some water or tomato sauce over them. Mix well to blend. Grab a handful of meat and round into a ball on your palms. Continue until all meat is finished.
5. Layer aluminum foil in bottom of roasting pan. Space meatballs on the top part of the roasting pan and broil about 5 min. on each side, until brown.
6. Add meatballs to pot with ribs and sausages. Simmer, covered 30-60 min., until ribs are tender.

7. **Prepare pasta:** Fill a large pot ¾ with water. Bring to a boil. Add 1 tsp. salt and when it boils again, add the pasta. Cook according to directions, al dente, 7 min.
8. Pour pasta in a large dish. Pour sauce over it and meat along the sides or in a separate dish drenched with sauce.
9. Serve with grated cheese.

# Meatless Meatballs – Polpette di Pane

The Italian word for meatballs is *polpette*. When I was a little girl in Italy, meat was scarce and expensive. My grandmother made polpette without meat but with bread and lots of grated cheese. The taste is so good that my relatives continue to make them as many times as they do those with meat. I recently ate polpette di pane while visiting my cousin, Rosaria on a trip to Italy. I didn't know there was no meat in it until she told me. That's how delicious they are! When she fries them, she spoons out a round mound of the mixture for each meatball and places it in hot oil, she said, because she doesn't want to dirty her hands.

*This is a great dish for vegetarians.*

## Ingredients:

10-12 slices of bread. Remove crust, if using Italian bread.

| | |
|---|---|
| 1 cup grated cheese | 3 eggs |
| ½ minced onion | 3 cloves garlic, minced |
| 1 tbs. parsley | 1 tsp. basil flakes |
| Some water or milk | Pepper to taste |

## Directions:

1. Wet bread with water or milk and let soak for 2-3 min. Squeeze liquid out of bread and place in a bowl.
2. Add other ingredients to bread and thoroughly mix with hands or fork. If too dry, add another egg; if too liquid, add more cheese. It will look like yellow cornmeal and should stick together.
3. Roll into round balls and place on broiling pan and broil on high for 4-5 min. until brown. Turn meatballs and do the same for other side. (Or, fry in a fry pan ¼ cup canola oil, which is lighter than olive oil and cheaper, until golden on both sides. Place meatballs on paper toweling to absorb oil.) Serve plain or with your favorite sauce.

# Sauces

# Basil Tomato Sauce, Meatless

When in a hurry and/or for meatless meals, this delicious sauce is ready in 10-15 min. Best with fresh, plum tomatoes and fresh basil leaves, but also good with canned tomatoes and dried basil flakes.

## Ingredients:

- 1-2 lbs. fresh, plum tomatoes
- 1 clove garlic, minced
- ¼ tsp. salt, pepper, rosemary, sage
- ½ cup fresh basil leaves or 2 tbs. flakes
- 1 onion, minced
- 1 tsp. parsley, minced
- ¼ cup olive oil

## Directions:

1. Heat olive oil in a large skillet on medium heat.
2. Add onions, sauté until brown. Add garlic, sauté 30 sec.
3. Wash tomatoes under water. Dice them and place in skillet.
4. Add spices, stir and cover. Let simmer for 15 min. stirring often, until tomatoes dissolve and form a thick sauce.
5. Pour over your favorite pasta and enjoy.

# Basic White Sauce

This is an alternate to red sauce and delicious for white lasagna or pizza or other pasta. *Adding 1 tablespoon of Parmesan cheese make this a perfect Alfredo sauce.*

Ingredients:
- 2 cubes butter
- 1 pint heavy cream, cold
- ½ cup of sweet white wine
- 1 tsp. garlic powder, optional
- 1 quart of half and half, cold
- 4 tbsp. corn starch
- ¼ cup chopped basil, optional

Directions:
1. In a bowl, whisk together the cornstarch with 2 or 3 tsp. cold water until well blended.
2. Melt butter in a fry pan on low. Add cornstarch paste and rest of ingredients and simmer for 3-5 min., until a semi-thick sauce is obtained.
3. Pour over your favorite pasta.

# Home-made Apple Sauce

Delicious with Turkey, Pork, Chicken or on its own as dessert.

Ingredients:
- 1 bag red delicious apples
- ½ cup water
- 1 tsp. or more cinnamon

Directions:
1. Rinse apples under running water. Peel and slice them. Drop them in a large pot. Sprinkle them with cinnamon (about 1 tbs.), then add ½ cup of water, cover and cook on medium heat for 20-30 minutes until slices are soft when touched with a fork. Stir to make a rough mixture.

# Pesto Sauce

You can buy pesto sauce, but it won't taste like the kind that's homemade. And it's so easy to do especially if you grow basil in your garden outside or indoors in a pot. You can also buy a bunch of fresh basil at the store any time of year. You can put parsley in the mix by using one cup of basil and one cup of parsley, if you prefer.

*Tip: If you double the recipe or make more, you can freeze what you don't use by pouring several spoonful (serving for one or two) onto a piece of waxed paper, fold closed and cover with aluminum foil. Place on a flat cookie sheet and put in freezer. Once frozen, place packages in a freezer bag, label and date and put back in freezer for future use.*

## Ingredients:
- 2 cups fresh basil
- 2 tbsp. pine nuts
- 3 chopped garlic cloves or more if you like it more garlicky.
- ½ cup olive oil
- 1/3 cup grated cheese

## Directions:
1. Wash basil and parsley, if using it, under running water. Dry with paper toweling. Cut off any thick stems.
2. Place oil, half of basil, pine nuts and garlic in blender or food processor and blend. Add remaining basil and blend to a fine texture. Puree.
3. Add cheese and blend quickly. Puree. Yields one cup ready to serve or freeze for a future time.

# VEGETABLES

# For Most Vegetables

Most vegetables (broccoli, string beans, zucchini, peas, asparagus, kale, swiss chard, mustard greens) can be made the same way and will taste delicious and retain their own flavor. I often mix two vegetables together (e.g., string beans and zucchini, broccoli and carrots, peas and carrots) to get more vitamins and minerals in my family's diet. I prefer to use fresh vegetables, but the frozen are good, too.

Ingredients:
- 1 or 2 fresh vegetables, rinsed
- 1/4 onion, minced
- ¼ tsp. or sprinkle of salt
- ¼ tsp. paprika
- Sprinkle of pepper
- ¼ cup olive oil
- 1 clove garlic, minced
- ¼ tsp. garlic powder
- ¼ tsp. basil flakes
- Sprinkle of white wine

Directions:
1. Rinse all vegetables under running water, peel and cut in pieces (carrots, broccoli skin) or snap off ends (string beans).
2. In a fry-pan, heat oil. Add onion and brown for 3-4 min. Add garlic for 30 sec., then the vegetables.
3. Add all spices and wine, stir, cover and sauté for 3-5 min., stirring a few times.

# Favas with Fennel

Fava beans need to be shelled and cooked but worth the effort. If you prefer or can't buy fava bean, substitute lima beans.

Ingredients:
- 1 lb. fresh fava beans, shelled
- ¼ cup diced pancetta or bacon
- 1 fennel bulb, trimmed, chopped
- 2 tbsp. lemon juice
- ¼ cup olive oil
- 1 onion, chopped
- 1 cup broth
- Salt and pepper

Directions:
1. To remove shells from fava beans, clean and boil them in a pot of water for 3-4 min. Drain, run cold water on them and open skins to remove beans.
2. Heat the oil in a pan, then, add the onions and fennel and sauté 3-5 min. Add the fava bean, ¾ of the broth, and simmer for 10 min. Add in pancetta and more liquid, if too dry. Simmer 15 min. more, until fava beans are tender.
3. Season with salt, pepper, lemon juice. Serve.

# Spinach or Broccoli Rabe

1. **With spinach**, first rinse all sand and dirt out of it by plugging up a clean sink, adding spinach and filling sink basin with water. Sand and dirt is heavier than the spinach and will sink to the bottom. With your hands, scoop up leaves and place in a colander to drain. Repeat 3 times to clean spinach thoroughly.
2. **With broccoli rabe**, cut thick ends and rinse the rest under water. Drain in a colander and then cut broccoli rabe sprigs in 2 in. lengths.
3. In a fry-pan, heat oil. Add garlic for 30 sec. Add the spinach (or broccoli rabe), some salt and garlic powder. Stir, cover and let simmer for 3-4 min. Spinach and broccoli rabe will reduce in size in seconds. Squeeze any excess liquid out with a fork through a colander but not all. The liquid contains many vitamins and mineral.

Broccoli Rabe

# Beets

1. Rinse beets under sink. Place in a pot of water, cover and boil for 30-60 min., until tender when pierced with a fork.
2. Drain cooked beets and let cool for a few minutes until you can peel off the skin with your hands.
3. Slice in a diagonal. Marinade with some salt and vinegar and refrigerate, or simply refrigerate as is or eat warm. Beets are delicious any way you serve them and they are rich in iron and add color to your table.

# Zucchini al Pregatorio

This is my cousin Lucia's recipe and it was delicious when she made it in her house near Milan.

Ingredients:

2 -3 large or 3-4 small zucchini    ¼ cup olive oil
2-3 cloves of cut up garlic    1 tbsp. white vinegar
1 tbsp. mint leaves    ¼ tsp salt

Directions:
1. Slice zucchini in round, thin circles to fill pan evenly.
2. Mix all other ingredients together and pour over pan.
3. Bake in 350 degree oven until soft, about 20-25 min.
4. Replenish with oil and vinegar as needed.

# Grilled (Really, Broiled) Vegetables

(They taste like sugar and the oil left on the cookie sheet after the vegetables are removed is delicious when rubbed with Italian bread. Easy to make, just a little time-consuming.

Ingredients:
- 1 eggplant
- 1 or 2 red or green peppers
- Salt as needed
- 1 or 2 zucchini
- Olive oil as needed

Directions:
2. Rinse the vegetables under running water. Slice peppers in half. Twist to remove stem and discard any seeds. Slice lengthwise about ½ in. wide.
3. Sprinkle olive oil on a large cookie sheet. Use a cut pepper piece to spread oil evenly.
4. Line up pepper pieces evenly on sheet. Lightly sprinkle salt and olive oil over each piece and broil on high for 5-7 min. until they turn brown.
5. With 1 or 2 forks, turn each pepper piece to the other side and broil 5-7 min. more.
6. While peppers broil, rinse eggplant and zucchini under running water, cut ends and, if much longer than the pepper pieces, cut in half horizontally. Now cut eggplant in half lengthwise and continue cutting in long strips to about same thickness and length of peppers.
7. Once peppers are done, remove from cookie sheet and place in a large bowl. Substitute eggplant in cookie sheet and repeat steps 3, 4 and 5.
8. Once eggplant is done removed from cookie sheet and add to peppers. Substitute zucchini on cookie sheet and repeat steps 3, 4 and 5.
9. When done, remove zucchini from cookie sheet and add to peppers and eggplant. Stir and the flavors blend into a delicious, healthy sweetness.

# Rice and Potatoes

Amalfi, Italy

# Rice with Onions and/or Curry

Rice is the easiest of dishes to make, but it can be made more flavorful with onions, spices and curry. You can also sauté mushrooms with the onions. Whatever suits you. If you don't have time to brown the onions, simply pour olive oil into rice when done.

## Ingredients:

- 1 cup rice
- 2 cups water
- ½ tsp. paprika
- 1 onion, diced
- ½ -1 cup mushrooms, optional
- 1 tbsp. olive oil
- ½ tsp. basil flakes
- ½ tsp garlic powder
- Pinch of salt

## Directions:

1. Boil rice according to package directions or add rice and water, bring to a boil, reduce heat to low and simmer 1 min. (minute rice) or 25-35 min. (brown rice). Let rest for 10 min.
2. While rice simmers, heat oil in a fry pan, add onions and brown 3-4 min., then cover to keep warm.
3. When rice is done, pour onions and olive oil and other ingredients in and stir with a fork.

# Risotto with Mushrooms and Zucchini or Peas

This rice recipe is more complex and takes more time and effort but it makes a delicious meal, even by itself. Mushrooms and/or zucchini enhance its flavor and nutrition. Serves 4-6.

## Ingredients:

| | |
|---|---|
| 4 cups clear broth | 1 oz. dry mushroom or 8 oz. fresh |
| 1 onion, chopped | 1 clove garlic, chopped |
| 1 cup Arborio rice | ½ cup white, dry wine |
| 2 small zucchini, diced | 1 tsp. sage |
| ¼ cup olive oil | 2 tbs. butter |
| ½ cup grated Parmesan cheese | Pinch of nutmeg |
| 1 tbsp. chopped parsley | 8 oz. frozen/fresh peas |

## Directions:

1. ***If you do not have broth ready, make it*** by putting 1 onion (peeled and halved), 2 stalks of celery and 2 peeled carrots in a large pot. Add 6 cups of water and bring to a boil. Cover loosely and boil for 1 hour to reduce liquid. Strain solids out and return clear liquid back in pot to stay warm for risotto.
2. ***If using dry mushrooms***, cover them with hot water to soak for 20 min. Strain and save the liquid.
3. Rinse and chop mushrooms.
4. In a large pot, heat the oil and sauté the onion on medium for 3 min. Add garlic and sauté for 1 min., then stir the rice in the oil and cook for 1 min. longer.
5. Add the wine, stirring until it is absorbed, then mushroom liquid, if any, until that is absorbed.
6. Now add zucchini or peas, stirring and repeating additions of broth, constantly stirring until it is absorbed and used up and rice reaches a creamy texture. Sprinkle with parsley and cheese and serve.

# Mashed Potatoes

Always feel free to add your creative touch. Add pepper or garlic powder or squeezed garlic or any other ingredient you like to make potatoes of your choice.

Ingredients:
    5-6 potatoes      ¼ cup milk
    ½ stick butter      Salt to taste

Directions:
1. Rinse potatoes. Place in a pot of salted water, cover and boil for 15-30 min., until tender when pierced with a fork. Drain and let cool for a few minutes until you can peel off the skin with your hands. Cut into smaller pieces.
2. Or peel skin off potatoes, cut potatoes into pieces and boil in salted water for 5-10 min., depending on size of pieces.
3. Place cooked potatoes in a mixer, add ¼ cup of milk, ½ stick (3-4 oz.) of butter and whip on high.

Bay of Sorrento, Italy

# Roasted Potatoes with onions

Ingredients:
- 5-6 potatoes
- ½ onion, chopped
- ¼ tsp. garlic powder
- ¼ tsp. basil flakes
- ¼ cup olive oil
- ¼ tsp. rosemary
- ½ paprika
- Salt to taste

Directions:
1. Peel skin off potatoes, cut potatoes into pieces or in the shape of French fries.
2. Place them in a large casserole.
3. Sprinkle top with onions, olive oil, salt, garlic powder, rosemary and basil flakes. Stir to coat potatoes with oil and spices.
4. Bake in a 400 degree oven for 15 min to cook and brown. Turn potatoes to other side to brown and continue cooking for 10-15 min. more.

# Quick French Fries

There are no ingredient amounts here because it depends on how many French fries you make. Remember that cooking is more an art than a science. Like good artists, good cooks don't always need measurements but use their eyes and fingers and eggshells, whatever they have available, to measure ingredients.

Ingredients:
    Potatoes                                  Olive oil
    Salt

Directions:
1. Take a large cookie sheet and coat the bottom with oil.
2. Peel and slice potatoes lengthwise like French fries.
3. Arrange them singly in the cookie sheet.
4. Sprinkle with salt and olive oil.
5. Place under broiler on high for about 5 min. until they brown.
6. With a fork, turn each fry to other side and broil until brown.

*Bonus: After you've eaten the fries, sop up the leftover oil on cookie sheet with bread.*

# Bread and Pizza

# Bread

For me, making bread is like going back to my childhood home in Italy, where my grandmother made the bread for our weekly consumption. She would mix the flour with the olive oil and yeast and knead it until it turned into fine silk. Like many people in the town of Castellaneta, she had no brick hearth to bake the bread, so she'd bring her lovingly-shaped loaves down to the local baker who had a wood-burning brick oven where he made pizza and baked bread for people in the town. Like my grandmother, and because it is a time-consuming process, when I make bread, I make enough to last a good week or more. So, as I combine the ingredients, knead the dough and shape it into my own rolls, I have my grandmother – Nonna- before me, smiling at me, loving me, watching me tweak her recipe with my own creativity.

## Ingredients

5 lbs. white unbleached flour       1 cup brown flour
3 tsp. salt                         1 cup olive oil
1 cup buttermilk or 1 cup milk with 1 tbsp. vinegar or yogurt
3 tbsp. granulated yeast            4 cups warm water

## Directions

1. Warm 4 cups water in the microwave, about 2 min.
2. Place yeast in a cup and fill with warm water to activate yeast. Let stand.
3. In a large bowl or pot, add both flours and salt. Make a well in the center and add the oil, working it in throughout the flour with your fingers.
4. Make a well again, add the buttermilk and work it through the dough.
5. Make a well a third time and pour in the yeast mixture. Work it through the dough. If some of the yeast remains in the cup, add some of the warm water and pour into dough. Repeat until the yeast cup is clean of yeast and water is used up.
6. Mix everything well, adding more warm water if too dry or flour if too sticky. *(To remove sticky dough from your hands, rub hands with some flour.)*
7. Turn onto a floured board or granite surface and begin kneading. Knead 5 to 10 min., adding more flour if

needed, until dough feels like silk, you hear it crackle and you see air pockets in the dough.

8. Gather it together into a ball and place it back in the large bowl or pot. Cover with a cotton dishtowel and place in oven heated to 170 F. Turn off oven and let rise for 1 to 2 hours, until double.
9. When risen, turn dough onto floured surface once more and punch down and knead 2-3 min. more. Cut small piece off and place rest in bowl and cover it.
10. Shape small piece of dough into a log. Cut into short sections, about 2 in. high and 2 in. long. Now shape each one into a thin log 7 to 8 in. long.
11. With thumbs and pointer fingers grab end closest to you and turn it over going forward and pressing down as you advance, creating a crescent roll.
12. Place on a cookie sheet sprinkled with rice flour or cornmeal (to prevent bread from sticking to cookie sheet during baking)
13. Repeat with rest of dough in a similar manner, spacing rolls on cookie sheet to give them enough room to double in size.
14. With a serrated knife, make a longitudinal slit about ¼ in. deep on each roll. Cover with cotton dishtowel and place in a warm oven to rise and double, about 20-30 min.
15. When double, remove dishtowel and raise temperature to 425 F. degrees and set timer for 14 min. Oven will probably take about 5-6 minutes to reach 425 degrees and bread should bake for about 8-10 min. at the high temperature to turn golden.
16. Now lower heat to 350 F degrees and bake another 8-10 min. (After 5 min., using a spatula, lift up one of the rolls and check that bottom isn't burning. If so, remove from oven as bread is done.)
17. Place on cooling rack or counter covered with wax paper or dishtowel to cool.
18. *Now here's the best part. When cool, wrap each roll with aluminum foil, place in a plastic bag and freeze. Take out a roll or two when and as needed and defrost in a warm oven for 5 min. or in the micro for 15 sec. each. The bread will taste as if you'd just baked it fresh that moment.* See photos that follow.

The Scent of Italian Cooking

# Irish Soda Bread

Perfect on St. Patrick's Day or any day. I learned this recipe from my Irish mother-in-law, who also taught me how to sew and how to cook basic meals.

Ingredients:

4 cups flour
3 tsp. baking powder
2 tbsp. caraway seeds
1¼ cup buttermilk or sour milk
1 tsp. baking soda

¼ cup sugar
1 tsp. salt
¼ cup butter
1 cup raisins

Directions:
1. Mix the flour, baking powder, sugar, salt and caraway seeds together.
2. Add butter and cut into flour mixtures with two knives. Stir in raisins.
3. In another bowl mix in whole egg, baking soda and beat. Mix with dry mixture.
4. Turn out to floured surface. Knead 5 min. until smooth.
5. Place in round, greased bowl. Cut an X on top of batter.
6. Bake in 375 F degree oven for 1-1¼ hour until golden brown. Test by inserting toothpick, which should come out dry when done. Remove from oven and cool 10 min. in pan. Then remove from pan for further cooling. Slice and enjoy.

*Tip: You can make your own buttermilk (sour milk) by adding a tablespoon of vinegar or lemon juice to 1 cup of milk.*

# Italian Easter Bread

Like the Christmas Trees Cookies that are part of our family's Christmas tradition, this Easter bread is part of our Easter tradition. I place one Easter bread loaf on each plate and it serves as a decoration as well as the bread for the meal.

Ingredients:
- 1 cup granulated sugar
- 5 eggs, lightly beaten
- ¼ lb. (1 stick) butter, melted
- 1 tsp. vanilla extract
- 6 raw uncolored eggs
- 1 egg, well-beaten for wash
- 6 cups flour
- 3 tsp. baking powder
- 1 cup milk
- 1 tsp. almond extract
- Multi-colored sprinkles

Directions:
1. In a large bowl combine sugar, baking powder and flour.
2. Make a well in the center and add the eggs with the melted butter.
3. Add the milk and flavorings and work the mixture into dough.
4. Roll dough into a log. Cut 6 equal portions. Using one portion at a time, remove ¼ of the dough and set it aside. Roll the larger portion into a horseshoe shape with the two ends facing you. Twist a loop at the top, leaving a space large enough to fit one egg. Continue twisting loosely until the end. Lay one raw egg in the loop formed by the dough.
5. Roll out the reserved dough into a 12-in. rope. Lay it over the egg and twist it the same way. Repeat with the remaining dough and eggs. Brush dough with the beaten egg and cover with sprinkles.
6. Place on a parchment-lined baking sheet and bake in a 350 F degree oven 25-30 min., or until dough is golden-brown. Makes 6 breads that look like the doll my grandmother taught me to make using a small towel.

# Pizza

There's nothing like home-made pizza. Once you have the dough, it's easy to make it. Set aside some of the bread dough, about 4 or 5 pieces of dough you'd use to make the rolls. You can wrap it in wax paper or plastic wrap, and again in aluminum foil and freeze it to make pizza at a future time or you can make it at the same time. If you freeze it, however, you should let it rise ½ hour, covered, in a warm oven before shaping into a round for pizza.

## Ingredients

- Dough
- Shredded mozzarella
- Other toppings of choice
- tomato sauce
- drizzle olive oil
- Rice flour/corn meal

## Directions:

1. Press with fingers to flatten dough into a circle.
2. Using a roller, start from circle center. Roll dough out all around until thin, even and to the shape/size of pan.
3. Dust pan with rice flour or cornmeal and place dough in it pressing with fingers throughout dough to fit into pan, rising a little at edges of pan.
4. Drizzle dough with olive oil. Evenly spread tomato sauce over it, keeping sauce ½ in. away from sides.
5. Sprinkle with mozzarella cheese and add other toppings, if desired.
6. Bake in a 400 F degree oven for 15-20 or until sauce and cheese bubble. Use a spatula, to lift dough and see if it's cooked through or needs more time. Slice and enjoy warm.

# Taralli

This is my mother's recipe and, as you can see, she always cooked in large quantities. You might want to cut the ingredients in half and still get plenty of taralli. You could also substitute some white wine for a portion or all of the water.

Ingredients:

2 lbs. flour (8 cups)  
½ tsp. salt  
12 eggs  
1 tbsp. of sugar  
1 eggshell of oil  
½ glass of water  

Optional (1 tbsp. anise or fennel seeds or black pepper added to flour)

Directions:
1. Beat eggs well, adding salt and water as you beat.
2. In a large bowl add flour and oil, mixing well, then, sugar and egg mixture.
3. Mix well and turn onto floured surface. Knead 5 min. until dough crackles.
4. Cut a small piece of dough and shape into a log, 6 in. long, ¼ in diameter.
5. Shape into a horseshoe, overlapping ends. Pinch ends together with finger or end of large old-fashioned key. Repeat steps 4 and 5 for rest of dough.
6. Gently drop each tarallo in a pot of boiling water. Do not over-crowd.
7. As soon as they rise to surface, remove tarali with a slotted spoon. Place on cookie sheet lined with wax paper.
8. Bake in 375F degree oven 15-20 min., until golden. Remove, cool.

# I Dolci – Desserts

## Gelati

# Biscotti

The word biscotti means, literally in Italian, twice cooked. The anise gives them that heavenly flavor and scent. They are delicious eaten plain, dunked in coffee or with ice cream. This recipe makes about 50 biscotti.

## Ingredients:

- 1 stick butter (4 ounces)
- ½ cup vegetable oil
- 1 ¾ cups sugar
- 6 eggs
- 1 teaspoon vanilla extract
- 1 cup of chopped dried fruit, optional
- 6 cups all-purpose flour
- ½ tsp. salt
- 3 tsp. baking powder
- 1 cup toasted almonds
- 2 teaspoons anise extract

## Directions:

1. If almonds aren't toasted, they can be toasted by layering them flat on a cookie sheet under broiler for about 1 minute until they start to turn slightly brown. Remove promptly or they will burn. Place on a wooden board and chop with a large (butcher) knife.
2. In a large bowl, cream the butter, oil and sugar together. Add eggs and beat until fluffy. Add vanilla and anise extracts and beat until blended.
3. Preheat oven to bake at 350 degrees F (165 degrees C).
4. Sift together the flour, baking powder and salt. Pour them into egg mixture and blend. Add chopped almonds and stir in with a spoon. Turn contents onto a floured board or granite top and knead by hand for 2 to 3 minutes until dough is firm. If dough seems too sticky, add a handful of flour; if dough is too dry, add a few drops of oil.
5. Divide dough into 4 equal sections. Roll each section into a log about 12 to 15 inches long and place on your cookie sheet, 2 to a sheet. Flatten top to reach a width of 2 to 3 inches, adjusting sides with your hands so width is uniform from end to end. Repeat with remaining sections.
6. Bake for 25 to 30 minutes until loaves turn lightly golden and feel firm to the touch. Place loaves on wooden board and with a sharp knife cut them into diagonal slices ½ inch wide. Gently pick up cut slices and return to cookie

sheet so that cut side is down. Place in oven for about 5-7 minutes to toast on one side, then turn them over to toast on the other side for another 5-7 minutes.

# Cartellate

This is the dessert of my hometown of Castellaneta. We made it with vino cotto (the boiled and reduced juice of dried figs), which is hard to get, except in Castellaneta. Each household made it for Christmas. Now many of my relatives have moved to other parts of Italy because of jobs. Still, they continue the tradition of making cartellate during Christmas time. Usually 2 or more relatives get together at one house and make it for that household. Then they go to the others' houses and do the same until everyone has an ample supply to carry them through the festive season. Cartellate last for several weeks, therefore they can be made in advance and stored in the warmest part of the refrigerato, or in a cool, dry place. The longer that they are stored, the softer they become. Serve room temperature.

Ingredients:
1 kilo (2 lbs.) flour (8 cups)   ¾ cup olive or canola oil
Pinch of salt   2 eggs
Pinch of carbonato (bicarbonate of soda)
½ cup white wine for consistency
Pinch of canella (cinnamon)
1 tbsp. flavored liquore, anisette, grappa, Sambuca limoncello
Vino cotto (the reduced juice of dried figs, boiled) or honey

Directions:
1. Mix all ingredients except vino cotto or honey.
2. On a floured surface, knead dough, 5 min., to soft, smooth consistency. If too sticky, add some more flour; if too firm, add some more wine.
3. Make dough into a long log and cut into small sections.
4. With a rolling pin, flatten dough into lasagna-slice thickness, 2 in. wide, 12 in. long; or pass through pasta machine on 1, 3, then, 5 and layer it on a board.

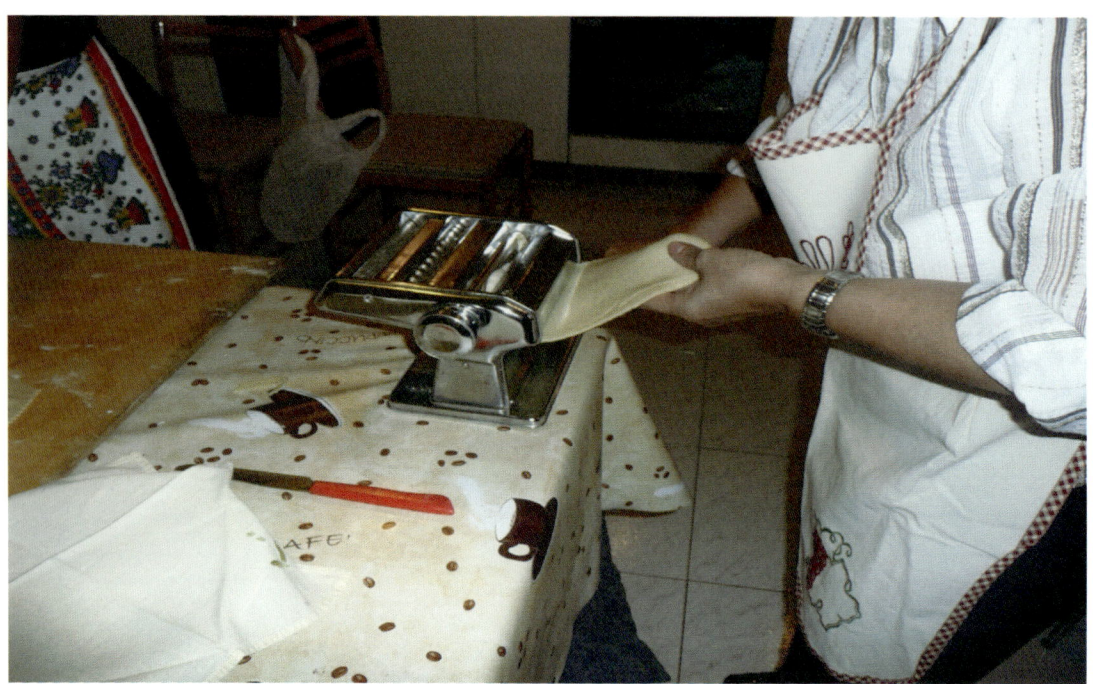

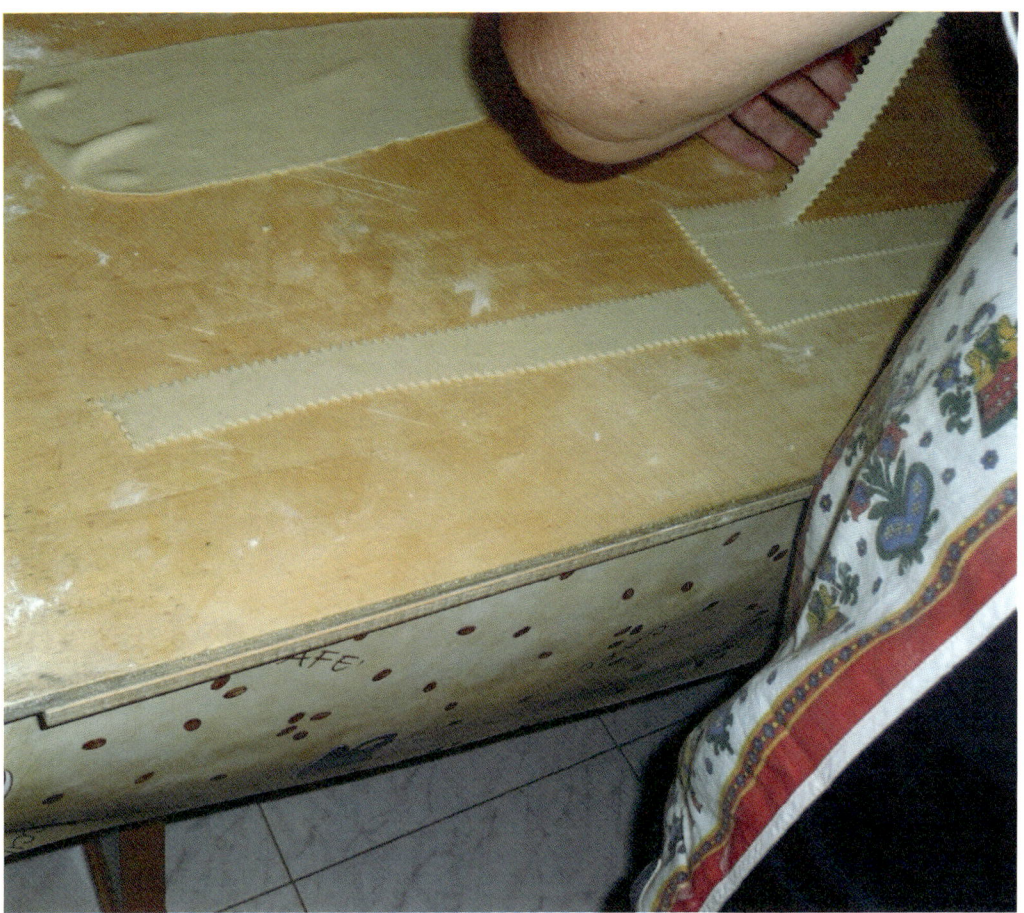

       Use scalloped pizza cutter to trim edges.
5. With your fingers, lift, fold and pinch opposite sides of dough 1 in. apart, creating pockets that will hold the honey.
6. Turn one end, twisting and pressing dough together with fingers in a circular fashion to make star or snow-shaped cartellata.

My cousin Lucia (right), a friend and I (left) shaping the cartellate, Lucia's house in Milan, Italy

Place finished cartellate on cookie sheet or wax paper. Repeat steps 4 to 6.

7. Heat about three cups of oil in a wide pot.
8. When oil is sizzling, drop cartellate in one at a time. Do only 3 or 4, or as much as the flat, inside surface area of the pot will allow. Cartellate rise to the top quickly, 1-2 min. Turn them gently once as they start to turn golden.

9. When golden, scoop out each one with a slotted spoon (spoon with holes) and place upside-down in a dish that's lined with paper toweling to drain oil.
10. Heat honey or vino cotto in a pot and dunk cartellate in. Remove with slotted spoon and straddle cartellate one over the other in a large dish or storage container.

Cartellate in pot of boiling oil

Cartellate ready to go into pot of boiling oil

Cartellate ready to enjoy

# Fritelle, Zeppole, or Pettole

So named, depending on the region of Italy you come from, these are pieces of dough, dropped and fried in oil, that come in different shapes of animals or objects and are fun to make especially with children, trying to guess what animal it looks like. They are a delicious dessert to eat with the whole family. In Castellaneta, we called them pettole.

## Ingredients:

4 cups flour
½ cup lukewarm water
Sugar or cinnamon for sprinkling
1 tsp. lemon or orange extract
½ tsp. salt
1 tsp. granulated yeast.
3 eggs (optional)
¼ cup muscatel, optional

## Directions:

1. Place yeast in a cup and water. Let it percolate.
2. Place flour in a bowl and add all the ingredients. Mix and knead to consistency of pancakes, adding more water or flour as needed. Cover and let rise for 1 hour in a warm place.
3. Fill a pot ¾ with vegetable oil and heat. Holding bowl near pot with hot oil, insert hand in batter, bring it over hot oil and let dough drip from fingertips into hot oil. Dough will rise, forming different shapes, turning golden in a few minutes.
4. Scoop out with a slotted spoon and place on paper toweling. Sprinkle with powdered sugar or cinnamon.

*Tip: Wet fingers in a small bowl of oil to coat them before picking up dough to drop in hot oil.*

# Torta di Mele

Torta means cake or tart. It's really Italian apple pie.

Ingredients:
- 2 tsps. Baking powder
- 1 cup sugar
- 2 tablespoons of olive oil
- 1 apple cut in long slices
- 12 oz. marmalade (prune or cherry)
- White sugar for sprinkling
- 1 lb. flour
- 1 stick butter softened
- 1 apple cut in pieces
- 3 or 4 eggs blended
- pinch of salt

Directions:
1. Mix all ingredients except marmalade and long-sliced apples. Pour ½ into cake pan.
2. Then add the marmalade. Then add rest of mixture.
3. Put long slices of apple around top.
4. Place in oven at 350 degree Fahrenheit oven (180 degrees Celsius) for 1 – 1 ½ hours, until golden. Check with toothpick. If it comes up dry, then it is done. Sprinkle with white sugar and serve.

# Oatmeal Cookies

Ingredients

- 1 cup flour
- ½ tsp. salt
- ¼ nutmeg
- 1¼ cup firmly packed brown sugar
- 1 tsp. vanilla
- 2 cups uncooked oats
- ½ cup nuts (optional)
- ¾ tsp. baking soda
- 1 tsp. cinnamon
- ¾ cup softened butter
- 2 eggs
- 1 tsp. almond extract
- 1 cup raisins (optional)

Directions:
1. Add butter, sugar, eggs and vanilla in a mixing bowl. Beat 2 min., until smooth.
2. Combine flour, soda, salt, cinnamon and nutmeg and add to egg mixture.
3. Stir in oats, raisins and nuts. Blend together with spoon.
4. Drop by heaping spoonsful onto greased cookie sheets.
5. Bake in preheated oven at 350 F degrees for 10-12 min. Makes about 36-40 cookies.

# Orange Cookies

Ingredients:

- 2 cups flour
- 2 tsp. baking powder
- 4 eggs
- ½ cup sugar
- ½ stick butter
- Zest of 1 orange & juice

Directions:
1. Cream eggs, sugar and butter in mixer, medium speed.
2. Add flour and mix on low.
3. Grate the skin of orange to make zest. Add to mixture.
4. Shape a spoonful of dough into a ball. Place balls on pan.
5. Bake in a 400 F degree oven for 8-10 min until golden.
6. Remove and place on a sheet of wax paper to cool.

# Christmas Tree Cookies

For these traditional Christmas treats, I use a cookie press that has a Christmas Tree plate that shapes the cookies. Not only does my family love them, but they come to expect them every year. It's not Christmas without them, they tell me.

Ingredients:
- 1 cup of butter (or half oil, half butter)
- 2 ½ cups of flour
- 1 tsp. baking powder
- 1 tsp. vanilla extract
- Green food coloring
- 2 eggs
- ¾ cup sugar
- ¼ tsp. salt
- 1 tsp. almond extract
- multi-colored sprinkles

Directions:
1. Cream butter and sugar well.
2. Beat in eggs and extracts.
3. Gradually blend in dry ingredients and tint the dough with 2 or 3 drops of food coloring. Mix well, using an electric mixer.
4. Place tree plate inside cookie press and fill it with cookie dough.
5. Form cookies on ungreased cookie sheet and decorate with sprinkles before baking.
6. Bake for 5-6 minutes in a 375 F degree oven. Remove from sheet and place on wax paper to cool. Cookies should be soft. They will harden some as they cool but taste best when not totally hard but semi-soft.

# Honey Balls (Strufoli)

Another Christmas Tradition. A little tedious to make, but let your children or grandchildren help with the rolling. They will love it and save you time.

Ingredients:

¼ lbs. butter (1 stick)
1 cup sugar
¼ tsp. salt
1 tsp. vanilla extract
1 large jar honey
2 cups of vegetable oil

4 cups flour
2 tsp. baking powder
4 eggs
1 tsp. almond extract
multi-colored sprinkles

Directions:
1. Cream butter, sugar, eggs and extracts. Mix in flour and baking powder.
2. Work dough, adding more flour if sticky, until it is smooth.
3. Cut dough into small pieces and roll out into ropes. Cut rope into dice-sized pieces and roll each one into a ball the size of a small marble and place on cookie sheets or wax paper.
4. Place vegetable oil in a shallow pot and bring to a boil.
5. Gently drop the balls a few at a time in the hot oil to boil for 1 or 2 min. until they rise to the top and are golden brown. Balls will have doubled in size.
6. Scoop golden balls onto a dish lined with paper toweling to absorb oil.
7. In another pot, heat about 2 cups of honey and gently add fried balls so they drench with honey. Scoop out balls and place on serving dish, piling them into volcanic-looking mounds. Apply multi-colored sprinkles all around honeyed balls. Once cool, cover with plastic wrap or decorative see-through wrap. Tie with colored string.

# Blueberry (or Raisin) Muffins

For raisin muffins, simply substitute raisins for blueberries, or use both in the same recipe, if you like.

Ingredients:
- 2 cups flour
- 1 cup blueberries, washed, dried
- ¼ tsp. salt
- ½ cup milk
- 1 tsp. vanilla extract
- 1 cup sugar
- 2 tsp. baking powder
- 1 egg
- 1 stick butter (½ cup)
- 1 tsp. almond extract

Directions:
1. Grease muffin pan or use paper muffin cups.
2. In a mixer, cream butter and sugar. Blend in milk, egg and extracts and change to a lower speed. Slowly add flour, baking powder and salt and blend together.
3. Add blueberries (or raisins) and mix with a spoon by hand.
4. Spoon batter into muffin cups, filling them ¾ of the way. Bake 400 degrees for 18-20 min., until muffins spring back when lightly pressed with finger. Serve warm or cold.

# The Paste of Royalty

Besides cartellate, this was my favorite sweet food when I was growing up in Italy. The taste is truly royal!

## Ingredients:

    1 lb. almonds                          1 lbs. sugar
    Juice from ½ lemon               food coloring
    Drops of different flavored liquors to match fruit flavors (Strega, Galliano, Limoncello, Triple Sec, Grand Marnier, etc.)

## Directions:

1. Put almonds in a pot, cover with water and boil until tender, 10-15 min.
2. Drain and run cold water over almonds to cool. Peel off almond skins.
3. Combine almonds and sugar in a bowl and mash finely to produce a paste.
4. Add lemon juice. Be careful not to make paste too soft.
5. Divide paste into as many balls as you have liquors and shapes you want to make.
6. Add appropriate liquor and food color to each portion to make fruit shapes, e.g. for lemons, use limoncello or Strega or Galliano plus a drop of yellow food coloring. Shapes can be strawberry, watermelon slice, orange, peaches, Banana, cherry, fig, tomato, etc.

# Apple Crisp

You can substitute pears, peaches, plums, apricots or use a combination of them. If you don't have all the spices and/or extracts, use or substitute what you have. Be creative and resourceful.

Ingredients:
- 5-6 apples, any variety
- 1 cup flour
- Pinch of salt
- 1 tsp. cloves
- 1 tsp. vanilla extract
- 1 stick of butter
- 1 cup oatmeal
- ¾ cup brown sugar
- 1 tsp. cinnamon
- 1 tsp. nutmeg
- 1 tsp. almond extract
- 1 tsp. lemon juice

Directions:
1. Peel and thinly slice apples. Place them in a buttered baking pan. Pour lemon juice over them to keep their color.
2. In a bowl, combine flour, brown sugar, oatmeal, spices, extracts and salt and blend ingredients together with a fork.
3. Cut butter in small pieces and blend with dry ingredients until mixture appears crumbly. Pour over the apples evenly.
4. Bake in a 400 degree oven for 10 min., then reduce to 350 and bake 15-20 min., until apples are soft when pricked with a fork and sides bubble. Serve warm or cold, with or without ice cream.

*Tip: Dot any dry areas with soft butter and sprinkle with cinnamon and lemon juice.*

# Apple Cobbler, Peach Cobbler, Pear Cobbler or Fruit Cobbler

Whatever fruits you have in the house, the more the tastier. You can even add nuts. If missing some of the fruit or extracts, not to worry. The cobbler still comes out delicious.

## Ingredients:

- 6-8 fruits, apples (pears, peaches, apricots)
- ½ cup blueberries
- ½ cup strawberries
- ½ cup of sugar (brown or white)
- 1 tsp. vanilla extract
- 1 tsp. anise and/or almond extract
- 2 bananas
- 1 cup of flour
- ½ stick butter
- ½ cup raisins
- ½ tsp. salt
- 1 tsp. cinnamon

## Directions:

1. Rinse all fruit under running water.
2. Peel apples and remove all stems and cores from all fruit.
3. Cut fruit in thin slices and line each fruit in greased pan, placing blueberries and strawberries toward the top, Raisins in the middle.
4. In a bowl, combine flour salt, sugar, spices. Cut butter into it to blend well and pour over top of fruit.
5. Bake in a 375 F degree oven for 20-30 minutes, until you see bubbling and fruit separates from the sides of baking pan. Drizzle with melted butter if top is dry.

**Cut fruit pieces before crumb mixture is added**

# Iced Apple Raisin Cookies

These were a favorite dessert for my children growing up, especially after school. The icing gives them a bridal appearance, but they are just as regal and delicious eaten plain.

## Ingredients:

| | |
|---|---|
| 1 cup diced, peeled apples | 1 cup moist raisins |
| 1 stick of butter (½ cup) | 2 ½ cups of flour |
| ¾ cup of white sugar | ½ tsp. baking soda |
| 1 tsp. baking powder | ½ tsp. allspice |
| 1 tsp. vanilla extract | 2 eggs |
| ½ tsp. salt | 1 tsp. cinnamon |
| 1 tsp. nutmeg | 1 tsp. cloves |

*For the Icing:*

| | |
|---|---|
| *2 cups confectioners' sugar* | *2 tbsp. milk* |
| *1 tsp. vanilla extract* | *1 tsp. almond extract* |

## Directions:

1. Combine flour, baking soda, baking powder, salt and dry spices in a bowl.
2. Cream butter, sugar, eggs and extract in electric mixer. Blend in apples, raisins and dry ingredients.
3. Place heaping, rounded spoonsful of dough onto greased cookie sheet.
4. Bake in 350 F degree oven for 5 min until semi-soft and golden. Cool.

*For icing: In a small bowl, add confectioner's sugar, milk and extracts. Consistency should be semisoft, like pancake batter. With a spoon or knife, gently cover top surface of cookies. Icing sets in minutes.*

# Plain Pastry for 2-Crust Pie

Ingredients:

|  | 9 inch Pie | 8 inch Pie |
|---|---|---|
| Flour | 2 cups | 1 ½ cups |
| Salt | 1 tsp. | ¾ tsp. |
| Vegetable Shortening | ¾ cup | 1/3 cup |
| Water | 1/3 cup | ¼ cup |

Directions:
1. Place flour in a bowl. Add half of shortening and cut it into the flour with a whisk, until the particles look like cornmeal.
2. Add remaining shortening and cut it in to the size of very small peas.
3. Sprinkle a measured amount of water over the sides of flour-shortening mixture a little at a time and blend inward with a fork, until all the particles are uniformly moistened and will barely stick together. Slightly more water may or may not be needed.
4. With one hand, gently press the pastry together into a ball. Cover bowl and let stand for 10 min.
5. Cut pastry into 2 equal parts. Take one part and turn to a flowered board or granite countertop and press with your hands to form a flat circle.
6. Using a roller, start from the center of the circle and roll out to the sides, working all around until pastry reaches 10 in. diameter and it is smooth.
7. Push a metal spatula under dough circumference to separate it from board or granite. With one hand, lift up dough from one side while the other hand pushes spatula further under toward the center to continue separating the round from the board.
8. Lay folded half over the other and continue pushing spatula under dough to separate it fully from board.
9. With both hands gently grab folded dough, supporting as much of it in your hands, and place it over pie baking dish so that its diameter is in the center of the dish and rounded edges lay on rounded edges of dish. Lift up top fold of dough and lay it across second half of dish. Dough should lay one inch down from pie dish edge. With scissors, cut off any uneven and excess dough all the way around. Patch up any areas that are short of dough by dabbing

some water on your fingers and wetting the dough. Place dough patch on it and press to adhere.

10. If making a pie that requires one crust, like pumpkin pie, lift edges of dough and, with fingers, crimp or squeeze it together all around so it makes a mini wall all around. Fill the middle with prepared filling and bake according to pie directions.
11. If making a pie that requires two crusts, like apple, fill bottom pie crust with fruit, then repeat steps 4 through 9 to make top crust. Now wet fingers with water and gently touch top edges of lower pie crust to moisten it.
12. Layer top crust over it the same way you layered bottom crust over pie pan. Fold top edges under and pinch together.

Street in Sicily

# Pumpkin Pie

Many people don't like pumpkin pie, but when they taste this one, they do. I substitute home-cooked pumpkin, left from Halloween which I freeze, and add vanilla and almond extract as well as allspice.

Ingredients:
- 2 slightly beaten eggs
- 1 ½ cups cooked pumpkin, pureed
- 1 cup sugar
- 12 oz. undiluted evaporated milk
- 9-inch single crust unbaked pie shell
- ¼ tsp. cloves
- ¼ tsp. nutmeg
- ¼ tsp. cinnamon
- ¼ tsp. allspice

Directions:
1. Combine eggs, pumpkin, sugar, salt and spices. Gradually add evaporated milk. Mix well.
2. Pour into unbaked pie shell where edges have been pinched or crimped to make a wall around pumpkin filling. Bake in 425 F degree oven for 15 min.
3. Reduce temperature to 350 degrees and bake about 40 min. more. (Knife inserted near center of pie should come out clean.) Cool before serving.

We often use pumpkin pie and apple pie as a birthday cake with candles for family members who have November birthdays celebrated on Thanksgiving Day.

# Apple Pie, Prince of Pies

Ingredients:

    Pastry for 9 in. double crust    2/3 cup sugar
    7-8 apples (different varieties)    1 tbsp. butter
    1 tbsp. flour    1 tbsp. lemon juice
    Dash of salt    ½ tsp. cinnamon
    1 tsp. vanilla extract    1 tsp. almond extract

Directions:

1. Wash apples, pare, quarter, remove cores and cut quarters lengthwise into 3 or 4 slices.
2. Blend flour, salt, sugar and cinnamon and sprinkle ¼ of mixture over bottom of pastry-lined pan. Stir rest of mixture lightly through apples and turn them into pan, arranging slices to fill shell compactly. Fruit should be slightly higher in the center.
3. Dot with butter and sprinkle with lemon juice, extracts and more cinnamon, if desired.
4. Moisten edge of lower pastry with fingers dipped in water. Add top layer and press down gently around edges to seal. Fold under pastry that hangs from rim of pan and crimp with tines of fork or pinch with fingers.
5. With serrated knife make an X on top center of crust to create opening for steam to escape. Bake 15 min. in a 450 F degree oven. Reduce heat to 325. Bake 35 min. or until apples are tender and juice bubbles out of vents. Cool or serve warm.

Apple pie used as a birthday cake on Thanksgiving Day

# White Icing

It's without milk or cream, perfect for anyone who is lactose intolerant. Frosting will last several months if stored in tightly covered container in refrigerator.

Ingredients:
- 2 cups of white veg. shortening
- ¼ cup egg whites (about 4 eggs)
- 1 teaspoon vanilla
- 1 cup 10X sugar
- 1 cup granulated sugar
- 1 tsp. almond extract

Directions:
1. In a mixing bowl, cream together shortening and confectioner's sugar.
2. Put egg whites and granulated sugar on top of double boiler. Place on stove over medium heat and beat to a stiff meringue as it heats.
3. Add half of meringue to bowl with sugar and shortening and beat on medium speed for 7-10 min.
4. Add rest of meringue and extracts. Beat 5 minutes longer until it forms stiff peaks.

View from my kitchen table on a summer afternoon.

# Cheese Cake

Ingredients:

3 large cream cheese (8 oz. each)    1 cup granulated sugar
1 and ½ tsp. vanilla extract    3 eggs
16 oz. sour cream    2 tbsp. granulated sugar
1& ½ cups graham crackers crushed    8 oz. butter, melted

Directions:

1. Place 1 cup of sugar and 1 package of cream cheese in a large mixing bowl. Mix at low speed. Add vanilla and alternate adding eggs and packages of cream cheese. Mix at medium speed for 5 min.
2. Add butter to crushed graham crackers, blend well with spoon to make a paste. Coat bottom and half of sides of one large spring-form pan (or baking pan or two 8 in. baking pans) with graham cracker paste. Bake in a 325 F degree oven for 8 min.
3. When done, place cream cheese mixture in pan or pans and bake again for 25 min. at 325 F degrees. Meanwhile, put sour cream and 2 tbsp. of sugar in a small mixing bowl. Mix at medium speed for 2-3 minutes.
4. When 25 min. of baking end, top cheese cake with sour cream mixture and bake again for 5 min.
5. Cool at room temperature and serve. Cover with wax paper and Reynolds wrap to store.

# Italian Cream

Ingredients:

6 eggs, separated
6 tbsp. flour
1 tbsp. cocoa, optional
1 tbsp. lemon peel, optional

2 cups sugar
4 cups of milk
1 tsp. vanilla extract

Directions:
1. Combine egg yolks, sugar and flour in a mixing bowl. Beat 3-4 min.
2. Warm milk in a pot on medium heat, stirring constantly. Pour half into egg mixture and beat 2 min. Pour rest in and beat 2 min. more.
3. Now pour egg mixture into milk pot and, under low to medium heat, bring to a boil, stirring constantly, until it thickens. Pour in a fresh bowl to cool.
4. Beat egg whites until stiff. Add to cooled cream and blend. Add cocoa or lemon peels and blend. Refrigerate or serve.

# Quick Icing, Vanilla or Chocolate

Ingredients:

½ cup butter
1 tsp. almond extract
2 cups confectioner's sugar
1 or 2 tbsp. cocoa powder or chocolate syrup (Optional)

1 tsp. vanilla extract
Pinch of salt
1 tbsp. milk

Directions:
1. Cream butter with sugar. Add salt, extracts and milk, (also cocoa or syrup for chocolate icing) and beat for 3 minutes on high speed.
2. If too thin, add more sugar; if too stiff, add a drop or two of milk. Frosts two 8 in. layers or 36 cupcakes.

# Course Index

## Appetizers

| | |
|---|---|
| Baked Clams | page 2 |
| Calamari Salad | page 3 |
| Fried Calamari | page 4 |
| Caponata Pugliese | page 5 |
| Frittata | page 6 |
| Tomato-Mozzarella | page 7 |
| Zucchini Pie | page 8 |

## Soups & Salads

| | |
|---|---|
| Chicken Soup | page 10 |
| Minestrone | page 11 |
| Pasta e Fagioli | page 12 |
| Green Salad | page 13 |
| Fresh Tomato Salad | page 14 |
| Italian Potato Salad | page 15 |
| Three Bean Salad | page 16 |

## Pasta

| | |
|---|---|
| Fettucini or other Fresh Long Pasta | page 18 |
| Gnocchi | page 19 |
| Lasagna | page 21 |
| Linguine with Muscles and Clams | |
| Marinara or White Sauce | page 22 |
| Linguine all Puttanesca | page 24 |
| Orecchiette | page 25 |
| Pasta with Cauliflower | page 27 |
| Spaghetti Carbonara | page 28 |

The Scent of Italian Cooking

## Pesce or Seafood

| | |
|---|---|
| Flounder, Grilled, Broiled, Baked | page 30 |
| Talapia, Grilled, Broiled, Baked | page 38 |
| Sole, Grilled, Broiled, Baked | page 30 |
| Swordfish, Grilled, Broiled, Baked | page 30 |
| Flounder, Talapia, Sole, Breaded | page 31 |
| Salmon Fillets | page 31 |
| Lobster | page 32 |
| Mahi-Mahi | page 35 |
| Salmon Fillets | page 31 |
| Shrimp, Barbecued | page 38 |
| Shrimp, Curried Rice and Veg. | page 36 |
| Shrimp, Pasta and Vegetables | page 37 |
| Shrimp Scampi | page 39 |

## Carne or Meat

| | |
|---|---|
| Barbecued Chicken | page 44 |
| Chicken Cacciatore | page 41 |
| Chicken in the Micro | page 45 |
| Chicken in the Oven (Baked) | page 42 |
| Chicken and Potatoes | page 46 |
| Chicken or Veal Parmesan | page 47 |
| Lamb Chops, Barbecued | page 50 |
| Osso Buco, Veal or Pork Shanks | page 53 |
| Pork Chops, Breaded | page 48 |
| Tomato Sauce with Meatballs, Pork Ribs, Sausage | page 55 |
| Meatless Meatballs (Polpetti) | page 57 |
| Turkey with Dressing | page 51 |
| Veal Saltimbocca | page 54 |

## Sauces

| | |
|---|---|
| Apple Sauce, Homemade | page 60 |
| Basic White Sauce | page 60 |
| Basil Tomato Sauce, Meatless | page 59 |
| Pesto Sauce | page 61 |

## Vegetables

| | |
|---|---|
| Most Vegetables | page 64 |
| Beets | page 67 |
| Favas with Fennel | page 65 |
| Grilled (Broiled) Vegetables | page 68 |
| Spinach or Broccoli Rabe | page 66 |
| Zucchini al Pregatorio | page 67 |

## Rice & Potatoes

| | |
|---|---|
| Rice, Onions, Curry | page 71 |
| Risotto with Mushrooms, | page 72 |
| Zucchini or Peas | page 72 |
| Mashed Potatoes | page 73 |
| Roasted Potatoes | page 74 |
| Quick, French Fries | page 75 |

## Bread (Pane) & Pizza

| | |
|---|---|
| Bread | page 77 |
| Italian Easter Bread | page 83 |
| Irish Soda Bread | page 82 |
| Pizza | page 85 |
| Taralli | page 86 |

## Desserts   Dolci

| | |
|---|---|
| Apple Cobbler, Peach Cobbler | page 105 |
| Pear Cobbler or Fruit Cobbler | page 105 |
| Apple Crisp | page 104 |
| Apple Pie | page 111 |
| Biscotti | page 88 |
| Blueberry or Raisin Muffins | page 102 |
| Cartellate | page 90 |
| Cheese Cake | page 113 |
| Christmas Tree Cookies | page 99 |
| Fritelle, Zeppole, Pettole | page 96 |
| Honey Balls (Strufoli) | page 91 |
| Iced Apple-Raisin Cookies | page 107 |
| Italian Cream | page 114 |

| | |
|---|---|
| Oatmeal Cookies | page 98 |
| Torta di Mele | page 97 |
| Orange Cookies | page 98 |
| Plain Pastry for 2-Crust Pie | page 108 |
| Pumpkin Pie | page 110 |
| The Paste of Royalty | page 103 |
| Quick Icing, Vanilla or Chocolate | page 114 |
| White Icing | page 112 |

My other cousin Peppino making mozzarella at home in Varese, Italy.